GOD CARRIED ME

A Testament to Faith Through Life's Storms

By Bertha Stumon

A Journey of Resilience, Loss, and Divine Grace

GOD CARRIED ME: A TESTAMENT TO FAITH
THROUGH LIFE'S STORMS

Published by: Ink Founders
ISBN: 978-1-970435-27-6

DEDICATION

To my son, **David Jerome Brooks**
Your brief life taught me the depth of love,
and your loss taught me the strength of faith.
You are forever carried in my heart.

To my Mother
Who showed me what it means to pray without ceasing,
to love without condition,
and to stand firm in the storms.
Your legacy of faith lives on.

To my daughter and grandsons
You are my sunshine after every storm,
my reason to keep standing,
and my greatest blessing.

To every soul who has ever whispered
"I don't know how I'll make it through"—
This is for you.
You are not alone.
God will carry you.

Table of Contents

AUTHOR'S NOTE

Dear Reader,

Before you turn these pages and walk with me through the storms of my life, I need you to know something: this book contains pain. Real, unfiltered, soul-deep pain. Within these chapters, you will encounter the death of a child, domestic violence, suicide, chronic illness, amputation, and grief that seemed too heavy for one person to carry.

If you are in a fragile place right now, please be gentle with yourself. If certain topics might be triggering for you, know that resources are listed in the back of this book. You are not alone, and help is available.

I did not write this book because my life was extraordinary. I wrote it because my God is extraordinary. Every chapter you are about to read is a testament not to my strength, but to His faithfulness. When my feet could not carry me, He did. When my heart shattered into pieces too small to gather, He held them all. When the storms raged with such violence that I could not see tomorrow, He walked me through the darkness step by trembling step.

This is not a book about how to avoid suffering. It is a book about how to survive it. It is about what happens when life brings Category 5 hurricanes to your door, and you have no choice but to stand in the wind and trust that God will not let you be swept away.

For too long, I kept my story locked inside, afraid that speaking my truth would be too painful, too raw, too much. But God kept whispering to my spirit: *"Your story is not just yours. It belongs to every person who thinks they cannot survive another day. Tell them. Tell them I carried you, so they will know I will carry them too."*

So here it is: my testimony, laid bare.

This book is for:

- Anyone who has buried a child and wonders if they will ever smile again
- Anyone trapped in an abusive relationship, wondering if escape is possible
- Anyone facing chronic illness and losing hope
- Anyone who has prayed and prayed and still not received the answer they wanted
- Anyone who whispers in the dark, *"I don't think I can make it through this."*

If that is you, this book is for you. And my prayer is that by the last page, you will know with absolute certainty that God can and will carry you through whatever storm you are facing.

Reading this book may be difficult. Some chapters will bring tears. Some will stir up your own memories of pain. But I also promise you this: you will see the faithfulness of God on every page. You will witness how He turns mourning into dancing, ashes into beauty, and weakness into strength.

You will see that survival is possible. That joy can return. That life after devastating loss is not just endurable; it can be beautiful.

My deepest hope is that this book does more than tell my story. I hope it becomes a mirror in which you see your own strength reflected back to you. I hope it becomes a map that shows you there is a path through the wilderness, even when you cannot see it yet. And most of all, I hope it becomes a testimony that when you are at your weakest, when your legs give out and your spirit falters, God will carry you.

He carried me through fire, through grief, through loss, through illness. He will carry you, too.

Thank you for trusting me with your time and your heart. May God bless you, keep you, and carry you through every storm.

With love and faith,

– *Bertha*

Prologue

The Anatomy of a Life Storm

The Vows of Survival

Every life, no matter how outwardly serene, inevitably faces its storms. But mine, I realize now, has not just weathered a few passing squalls; it has seemed, at times, to dwell permanently in the path of the relentless hurricane.

These were not simple inconveniences or brief moments of sadness. They were Category 5 disasters of the soul, the kind that don't just threaten to damage, but that can seemingly destroy everything in their path, leaving behind only debris, silence, and an echoing absence where hope once stood. I have tasted the bitter ash of profound loss, and I know the feeling of standing precisely in the center of the vortex, deafened by the wind's roar, watching as everything I admired was ripped away.

My stability, my physical health, the innocent expectation of a normal life, the very foundation of my family; all were threatened. The ground beneath my feet was never solid; it was perpetually shifting, soaked, and treacherous. I learned early that the world offers no guarantee of calm.

Yet, this book is not a tragedy, nor is it a lament. It is a powerful, living testament to survival, and more importantly, to resilience. It is a profound exploration of how the unrelenting floodwaters of those storms ultimately strengthened me. The forces that were supposed to break me, that should have reduced me to dust, became the very steel of my character. The scars I carry are not marks of victimhood; they are the topographical map of my victories. They chart the arduous journey of a woman who was knocked down but absolutely refused to stay down.

Through every punishing gust of wind, every heart-stopping clap of thunder, I pushed forward. I always found myself standing, sometimes barely, at the end, gazing back at the wreckage of what had been. And every single time, I arrived at the same disbelieving, humbling, and foundational question: *How did I possibly make it through that one?* The answer is the purpose of this book: **God carried me.**

Stepping Into the Eye of the Storm

I invite you now to step into the very *eye of a storm* with me. I want you to understand the raw, terrifying force I contended with, because without understanding the depth of the darkness, you cannot truly appreciate the brilliance of the light that follows.

Feel the terrifying wind blowing against your face, the kind that threatens to peel the skin from your bones and steal the breath from your lungs. Let the sound of the world dissolving into a ceaseless roar fill your ears. This is the soundtrack of helplessness, where human effort feels pointless. Wonder with me how long the downpour will last, and let the sickening panic of uncertainty settle deep in your bones. Understand what it means to be utterly helpless, stripped of all earthly control, facing a force that is simply bigger than you. This is the truth of the storm. This is where many people lose their way, succumbing to the cold, magnetic comfort of despair.

But I urge you to stay. Stay to witness the inevitable calm that follows, the quiet moment when the sun tentatively, shyly, breaks through the clouds. Stay to witness the enduring survival that follows, the slow, agonizing, but ultimately glorious process of rebuilding. Stay to see the woman who emerged; not merely surviving, but thriving; not just intact, but immeasurably stronger.

The resilience I discovered was not a natural talent or an inherited trait. It was a strength born of one, singular, constant truth: an **unshakable Faith in God.**

The Anchor of Unshakable Faith

To say one has faith is easy, often reserved for Sunday mornings or moments of gentle prayer. To live by it when the very foundations of your life are violently shaking is an entirely different reality. My faith was not a philosophical idea; it was a spiritual necessity. It was not a fragile umbrella offering minimal shelter; it was the heavy, tested anchor that held me fast to the bedrock of my spirit when the tides of grief, sorrow, and devastation tried to pull me under forever.

In the moments of deepest, most unbearable loss, the loss of family, the loss of my own physical well-being, there was nowhere else to turn. Human solutions failed. Therapy, money, the love of friends; they could all offer temporary comfort, but they could not heal the existential wound left by a major life storm. Only God could.

In the very moment of greatest desperation, I found the deepest peace. When I was physically and emotionally crippled, unable to take another step, I felt a strength that was not my own. This is the miracle of being carried. It is the profound, undeniable experience of realizing that when your own two feet give out, a greater, supernatural power lifts you. It is the awareness that the hands wiping your tears are divine, and the voice whispering, *"You are going to make it, my child,"* is the Creator Himself. This realization became the central pillar of my existence, the absolute truth against which all other storms would be measured.

The biblical Psalms speak of God being our refuge and strength,

"a very present help in trouble. Therefore, will not we fear, though the earth be removed, and though the mountains be carried into the midst of the sea" (Psalm 46:1-2).

That passage was my literal reality. The earth *was* removed. My personal mountains *were* shaken. But because of the refuge I found, I did not fear. I could not. When you are being held by the Creator of the universe, the storm, for all its terrifying power, loses its final, fatal authority over your soul. It can hurt you, but it cannot destroy you. It can wound you, but it cannot consume you.

This book is a deep dive into the practical application of this spiritual resilience. I define it not as *bouncing back*, as you never return to who you were before the storm, but as *bouncing forward*. You emerge as something new, denser, harder, more capable of enduring the next blow, yet softened by a profound empathy for others' suffering.

PART ONE
THE FOUNDATION STORMS

Chapter 1

The Foundation Storms (1950s - 1960s)

This first chapter is where that resilience began. It is the story of the earliest tempests that forged me, the storms of childhood that were entirely disproportionate to my ability to handle them. They were not just emotional; they were literal, physical, and educational setbacks that threatened to determine my course before I even had a chance to choose it.

The Country Roots: Setting the Stage for Endurance

My early years were spent on a modest, working farm in the deep country, an environment that was both a sanctuary and a relentless taskmaster. My world consisted of my parents, my dear grandmother, and my two brothers. Across the dirt road lived my four boy cousins, making me the only girl often playing with six rambunctious boys. This dynamic, while frustrating for them, taught me my first lessons in negotiating, standing my ground, and holding my own. I was the keeper of their secrets and their reluctant snitch; I would tell on everything they did!

My father was a dedicated man of the earth, an unyielding farmer who coaxed life from the soil with his own two hands. He grew the staples that fed the family and defined our livelihood: cotton, peas, corn, sweet potatoes, sugar cane, and a variety of other vegetables. There were no holidays or weekends off; the farm demanded every hour of our waking lives.

We all had to help out: my mother, my brothers, and I. It was very hard work, demanding a physical toll that began before the sun rose and lasted well after it set. We labored in the fields under the punishing

Southern sun, learned the rhythm of planting and harvest, and knew the ache of weary muscles before we understood the concept of leisure.

As the little sister and the only girl, my brothers were relentless. They insisted I pull my weight, demanding I do the exact same rigorous work they did. There was no special treatment in the fields, only the sweat and the sun. This unrelenting, demanding life was the very ground upon which my foundation was built; a foundation of tenacity, grit, and endurance that would prove indispensable when the real storms began to roll in. This relentless work ethic was the first unwritten lesson in survival: *If you don't work, you don't eat. If you don't endure, you don't survive.*

Storm 1: The Wind of Responsibility (My Mother's Stroke)

The first life-altering storm I registered was not the rain, but the crushing weight of sudden, unexpected responsibility. It began when my mother had a stroke. It was not a slow illness; the initial impact hit me with the force of a sudden, disorienting clap of thunder. Our entire domestic universe tilted on its axis, and the gravitational center of our home shifted violently.

My mother, the tireless engine of our household, was suddenly incapacitated. The very core of my childhood security, her hands, her voice, her presence, was gone.

The rain began falling hard because I was suddenly forced to take on her formidable obligations in the home. I had to become the stand-in mother and housekeeper. The wind was blowing hard, so I had to assume her role inside the house, managing the cooking, the laundry for the entire family, the cleaning, and the difficult task of caring for my sick mother and my elderly grandmother. *And* I was still required to work in the field.

By then, the storm had picked up speed and was in full, frightening force. I was just a young girl encountering this sudden deluge of adult responsibility, and I felt utterly inadequate. I didn't know how to navigate the kitchen, the complexities of cleaning a country house, or the sheer weight of a household's survival. It was too much for my small shoulders, and the fear of failure was almost as painful as the work itself. What if I couldn't cook? What if I made my mother worse?

In that moment of total overwhelm, with the weight of the entire family pressing down, I did the only thing I knew to do: I turned to God. I closed my eyes in the middle of the kitchen whirlwind and asked Him, not for the storm to stop, but to show me how to do the task. I asked Him to equip me for the role my mother had done. I sought His wisdom where my own knowledge failed. This act, this deep, desperate reliance on a power greater than myself, was the moment my faith evolved from a childhood routine into a true anchor.

I encountered that storm as a young girl, learning that dependence on faith was not a last resort, but my first and most powerful resource. I learned to pray while I was stirring the pot, to ask for guidance while I was scrubbing the floors. God was my co-pilot in the mundane and the impossible.

Soon, as my mother began the slow, arduous process of recovery, I was able to breathe easier. I had endured the first blast and, remarkably, the house had not fallen apart. I felt the palpable, undeniable presence of God in the quiet moments, a gentle, sustaining force that transcended the storm. I knew, with a certainty that anchored my soul, that He was the one who had carried me through that initial tempest, setting the precedent for every hardship to follow. I was not alone.

Storm 2: The Mighty Storm of Pain (The Fire Pit Accident)

The next significant storm that rolled in brought with it a literal, physical fire. It was a cruel irony that followed the hard-won sense of accomplishment from managing the household.

It happened on a long summer day after a grueling morning of laundry, a monumental task in those days. Doing laundry then was an immense, multi-step chore, and it included boiling the white clothes in a massive wash pot situated over a roaring fire outside, a process of boiling water and lye soap that demanded constant supervision. Finally finished, I went inside for what I felt was a well-deserved rest. I was absolutely exhausted, my small body weary from the labor.

After a little while, my brothers called for me to come outside. When I stepped out, my oldest brother was laughing; a sharp, teasing sound that should have been a warning. Confused, I asked why. He told me to go feel the water in the wash pot, claiming with a deceptive grin that it was barely warm.

In that moment of trusting innocence, everything went white-hot. As I walked toward the pot, I stepped directly into the hot ashes and the fire pit surrounding the wash pot. My right foot was instantly covered by the smoldering ashes and the residual heat. The result was a catastrophic injury: **third-degree burns.**

This storm struck with a violent, instantaneous force that was utterly consuming. The mighty storm of pain was so intense it was paralyzing; I couldn't move, couldn't think, could only register the agonizing fire consuming my flesh. The world reduced itself to an agonizing throb that consumed my entire awareness.

I was laid up, immobile, unable to bear weight on the foot. The long days of summer blurred into weeks of excruciating healing. The physical pain was a constant, vicious enemy, but it was compounded by a deeper fear: the fear of being permanently crippled. The severity of the injury was not lost on me, even as a child.

And then came the next crushing wave: the realization that the school year was about to start, and I was faced with the devastating reality of missing it entirely. My body, which was supposed to be my tool for work and for life, had betrayed me, and my immediate future was now forfeit.

Storm 3: The Downpour of Disappointment (The Education Setback)

The school year began, and I was a prisoner of the house for the entire first semester, trapped by my own injury. The rain was falling so hard outside, and I was crying just as hard inside, devastated that I couldn't join my fellows in the classroom. Education was never just a requirement for me; it was my dream, my escape, and the key I knew I needed to unlock a life beyond the farm. Now, that door was locked, and I was falling further and further behind.

When I finally returned to school, walking gingerly on my still-healing foot, I was met with an overwhelming downpour of *systemic disappointment*. The teacher, a figure who was supposed to be a source of encouragement, sat me down and told me plainly that I could not catch up. She did not believe it was possible to make up an entire semester of work, especially with my prolonged physical limitations.

The wind of that devastating judgment blew non-stop, threatening to flatten my self-esteem. Her decision was final: I had to repeat the fourth grade. She concluded that my prolonged absence meant I simply couldn't succeed in fifth. This was a profound, public blow. It was not just a repetition of a grade; it was a societal declaration that I was behind, less capable, and destined to struggle. It was a judgment based on circumstance, not competence.

I remember the shame, the tears, and the fierce, quiet determination that ignited in my chest. Still at that young age, I reached for the only source of comfort I knew. I felt the comforting, powerful presence of God actively calming the storm of my deep disappointment. I turned the humiliation into motivation. I realized God was not telling me to accept the judgment; He was empowering me to overcome it.

I spent a year and a half in the fourth grade, but instead of allowing that decision to define me as slow, I allowed it to define me as determined. I used that extra time not as punishment, but as preparation, mastering every subject until I was not merely caught up, but academically ahead. I was resolved to show them, and I did. I proved how smart I was, very smart indeed, graduating that grade not with a sense of failure, but with a victory banner in my heart.

Even with the many tears and the lingering physical pain from my injury, I was able to rise and survive. I knew, with absolute certainty, that God carried me through that foundation storm. He continued to sustain me, turning the disappointment into a powerful testament of resilience. I rose up, and I was able to live with it, carrying the steel of that early strength into every new challenge that life would inevitably bring. The woman who faced the future was forged in the heat and the flood of those first foundational storms.

The Lessons Forged in the Fire

The three storms of my early life, the Stroke of Responsibility, the Fire of Pain, and the Downpour of Disappointment, created the bedrock of my character. They were not isolated incidents; they were a foundational trilogy of endurance. This foundation, built on a swamp of despair and held firm by an anchor of faith, prepared me for the far greater tsunamis that lay ahead. It taught me the language of prayer, the necessity of grit, and the quiet truth that no matter how hard the rain falls, the sun will always be waiting.

The Foundation Storms have ended, but the journey has just begun. I am ready to move from the fields of my youth to the next season of life, where the stakes will be higher, and the losses will be far more devastating. I hope you will continue with me.

Chapter 2

The Next Season: Bouncing Forward

The woman who faced the future was indeed forged in the heat and the flood of those first foundational storms; the early trials of responsibility, physical pain, and educational setback. But a foundation is not a finished house; it is merely the ground upon which the true structure is raised. The next season of my life, the years defined by the dust of the country road and the polished hallways of the school system, would test that foundation further. It was here that I learned to accept the inevitable challenges not as punishments, but as crucial equipment for the far greater, more complicated Life Storms I was yet to face.

The foundation was grit. The next lesson was adaptability.

The Old School House

My early school life began in a place that felt like an extension of the farm itself: a small, unassuming building where the echoes of childhood laughter blended with the scent of chalk dust and worn wooden floors. This was not a sprawling campus but a single-structure sanctuary that housed every student from first grade right up to eighth grade. We were all together, a small, tightly knit community of country kids, most of whom knew each other's families and lived within a stone's throw of a cotton field or a cow pasture. The teacher was not just an instructor; she was an overseer of our small world, capable of teaching basic arithmetic to a six-year-old and preparing a fourteen-year-old for high school with equal authority.

Life in that school was predictable, a quiet, reassuring rhythm that mirrored the planting and harvesting cycles of the farm. We knew the faces, the routines, and the expectations. After the tumult of the Fire Pit Accident and the forced repetition of the fourth grade, this steadiness was a balm to my spirit. I had proven my academic worth; more than proven it, in fact, and now I could be absorbing knowledge and enjoying the fleeting calm before the next atmospheric pressure shift.

But as I had learned before, the world offers no guarantee of calm. The very moment you settle into the routine, the very moment you think you know the landscape, the winds of change begin to stir.

The Storm of Relocating

The first gust came not from nature, but from a bureaucratic decision far removed from our quiet country existence. The school system, in a move they termed consolidation or efficiency, decided to combine two existing schools. Our beloved, small building was one of them. We were to be combined with another school, located in *Grand Cane, Louisiana.*

When the news was announced, I remember the air in the classroom growing thick and still, heavier than the humidity before a summer rain. The older students exchanged nervous glances, and a low, unsettling murmur swept through the room.

The physical distance of the relocation, fifty miles away from the school I knew, was jarring enough, but the true impact was emotional. This was the moment the wind of uncertainty started farming and blowing hard across my personal landscape.

Fifty miles. It may not sound like much now, but to a girl who rarely ventured beyond the local church and the dirt roads surrounding the farm, fifty miles was a trip to the moon. It was an entry into the unknown, a journey across a foreign border. I was afraid of what it would be like at a new school. Would the teachers be kind? Would the work be harder? Would I, the girl who had already been publicly labeled as *behind* once, be able to catch up again in a completely new environment?

This fear was not merely about academics; it was about survival. My self-worth, which had been so arduously rebuilt in the wake of my injury, felt suddenly vulnerable again. The foundation of tenacity and grit I'd forged was being asked to support a structure in motion, a building lifted from its familiar ground and transported across the map.

What if I was not enough for this new challenge? That question, whispered by the gusting wind, was the most frightening part of all.

The Thunder and the Sun

Having to move to another school fanned another storm entirely: the storm of relocating. I heard the thunder rolling, and it shook me up with the simple, terrifying thought of leaving behind everything that felt safe and familiar. My stomach churned with every clap of that distant thunder, visualizing the loss of my known routine and the forced integration into a new social order.

I tried to use the lessons from my mother's stroke and the fire pit accident. I closed my eyes and whispered, *God, carry me. Just show me how to do this one thing.* But this time, the fear was less about physical pain and more about social anxiety; a fear that felt more internal and harder to fight.

Yet, as with all storms, this one eventually moved on. We arrived at the new school. The halls were different, the faces were new, and the logistics of the fifty-mile commute necessitated an entirely new schedule. But after the thunder, the lightning, and the rain passed, I realized that it was not as bad as I thought it would be.

The moment of realization was not a sudden, blinding flash of light; it was a slow, gradual warming, like the feeling of the first sunbeam hitting your face after days of rain. I settled down. I found my classes, found a desk, and found, much to my relief, that children, even fifty miles away, were still just children. My academic determination, which had been hardened by the teacher's skepticism, allowed me to quickly regain my footing. The sheer grit that was necessary to work a farm before dawn and then focus on schoolwork was not lost in translation; it was merely applied to a new setting.

I started enjoying the sunshine after the storm. The new environment, instead of being a hindrance, became a catalyst. It forced me to stretch my social boundaries, to engage with unfamiliar perspectives, and to strengthen that muscle of adaptability. The relocation was not a loss of my old self, but a necessary expansion of my future self. I bounced forward not only with my education intact, but with the quiet confidence that I could handle a sudden, major shift in location or circumstance. This was the first great lesson of my next season: change, no matter how terrifying the initial wind, is an opportunity for growth.

The Cold Wind of Difference

The relative calm of the consolidated school was short-lived, replaced by the fierce, complicated storm of adolescence: high school.

Once again, it was a new life of changes, but this transition felt far more charged than the fifty-mile move. High school was the crucible where my country roots were truly tested.

I was, fundamentally, a student who came from the country. My hands were familiar with the feel of rough cotton bolls and the smooth, wet handle of a shovel. My clothes, while clean, carried the faint, persistent scent of field work and lye soap. I walked with the purposeful stride of someone who had spent her early life moving fast to keep up with men twice her size, and I carried the quiet, self-sufficient reserve of someone who knew the value of hard labor.

The irony, and the difficulty, was that most of the other students were also from the country, or at least from the small towns surrounding the high school. Yet, within the delicate, unforgiving social hierarchy of a high school, a subtle, but brutal distinction existed: there were country kids, and then there were *farm* kids, and I was the latter.

The kids whose parents worked at the local store or had a profession in the nearby town looked upon those of us who came directly from the dirt roads and cotton fields with a kind of gentle, yet cutting, disdain. I was not easily accepted, only because I came from the country. The way I spoke, the way I dressed, the simple fact of my parents' livelihood, it all marked me as an outsider, someone perceived as less sophisticated, perhaps even less intelligent, than those who hadn't spent their childhoods in the relentless, demanding cycle of agricultural labor.

This was not a Category 5 hurricane, but a persistent, biting wind, the wind of social exclusion. It was not loud; it was subtle, the kind of quiet judgment that freezes the soul far more effectively than a sudden blast of anger. It felt like being placed under constant scrutiny, where every action was weighed and measured against an invisible, arbitrary scale of acceptance.

The Strength to Stand

The wind blew, and instead of allowing it to knock me down, it stoked a familiar, righteous fire in my belly. I realized quickly that the only currency that mattered, the only shield I could wield against the societal declaration that I was *less than*, was my mind.

If they thought I was a simple farm girl, I would prove them wrong by becoming the smartest student in the room.

The battle was not fought in the hallway; it was fought in the classroom and in the late hours spent over textbooks. I had to prove that I was as smart as the next student if taught the same thing. This was the ultimate realization: my intelligence was not defined by my postal code or the mud on my boots; it was a fundamental, God-given capacity, and all I needed was the opportunity to unleash it.

This period was characterized by a relentless internal struggle. The sheer exhaustion from balancing farm chores with rigorous high school demands was immense. I remember nights when the pressure felt almost physical, the weight of expectation; both my own and the unspoken judgment of my peers pressing down on my chest.

In the rising of this storm, I had to fight through the wind and the rain to prove that I could weather the storm. The wind whispered doubts: *You're just a farm girl. You'll never go anywhere. This is too hard.* The rain was the constant tears of frustration when a concept didn't click immediately, or the hurt from an overheard, dismissive comment.

It was the strength from God that allowed me to withstand the storm. My faith, which had evolved from a simple Sunday routine to a necessity during the earlier tempests, became my strategy. I didn't just pray for good grades; I prayed for clarity, for endurance, and most importantly, for the wisdom to see my own worth independent of human judgment.

I truly depended on God to carry me through. I was keenly aware, even in those moments of academic struggle and social pain, that this struggle was not just for me. My resilience was being hardened and refined so that I could be able to help someone else through their storm one day. Every late night spent studying was not just about passing a test; it was about laying the groundwork for a testimony.

The Sunlight of Victory

Slowly, steadily, the hard work bore fruit. My grades were not just good; they were excellent. My teachers, recognizing the depth of my dedication and my undeniable intellect, began to champion me. The very students who had once dismissed me began to look to me for help with their assignments. The currency of social acceptance shifted from my physical origins to my intellectual capability. The silence of exclusion was replaced by the request for collaboration.

This acceptance, earned through sheer merit, allowed the sun to start peeking through the rough clouds in other areas of my life. I joined the basketball team in high school. Basketball became the dynamic, physical outlet for all the pent-up tenacity and grit I had developed working in the cotton fields. It was not just a sport; it was a visible declaration of my strength and coordination.

We won many championships. The feeling of unity with my teammates, the collective effort, the roar of the crowd, it was a glorious, undeniable sensation of belonging. Every basket, every win, chipped away at the old stigma and affirmed my place, not just as a student, but as a leader.

My newfound identity was celebrated publicly. Every year for the homecoming, I was in the parade. Riding on a float, waving to the crowds, was a far cry from sweating in the fields under the relentless Southern sun. It was a tangible, beautiful symbol of bouncing forward, not just surviving the storm of exclusion, but stepping out of the wreckage and into the light of recognition. The girl who was deemed "behind" was now, clearly and unequivocally, *ahead*.

A Moment of False Calm

The momentum was unstoppable. I graduated from high school with academic honors and the confidence of a champion. After graduation, I was accepted into college, a long-awaited realization of my dream, the ultimate key to unlocking a life beyond the rigorous demands of the farm. I felt the powerful, exhilarating promise of an open future, a horizon unclouded by the judgment of others or the limitations of circumstance.

I started college the following September. The first few months were intoxicating. The campus was vibrant, the subjects were challenging, and the taste of independence was sweet. I was navigating a new city, handling a demanding academic load, and thriving in the freedom of making my own choices. I thought I had weathered all the major storms and that the rest of my life would be a gentle, steady sail.

But the very act of choosing my own path brought me face-to-face with the most dangerous kind of storm: the self-inflicted deluge.

The Wrong Choice and the Dark Clouds

It happened quietly, almost without fanfare. At the end of the year and the beginning of the semester, I learned I was pregnant.

The realization didn't hit me with the force of an external hurricane, but with the quiet, sickening certainty of a foundation crumbling from within. This was a storm I had brought on myself by making the wrong choice. Unlike the stroke, the fire, or the forced relocation, events that were external and beyond my control, this one was entirely my own doing.

The shame and the guilt were immediate, heavy, and suffocating. The shame was not about the physical reality; it was about the disappointment. I had worked so hard to prove my worth, to earn my place in college, to become the exception; the girl who *left* the farm, the one who *made it*. And now, in a single moment of poor judgment, I felt I had risked throwing it all away.

I continued to go to my classes until the very moment I went into labor. This was an act of sheer denial driven by terror. I was desperately trying to hold onto the illusion of normalcy, clinging to the routine of lectures and textbooks while a profound, life-altering reality grew inside me.

The silence I kept was a pressure cooker of internal anxiety. I had many dark clouds of disappointments, but the deepest darkness came

27

from not knowing what to do or what to say to my parents. My mind replayed every hopeful conversation we had ever had about my future, every proud look my father had given me when I came home with good grades, every dollar they had sacrificially spent on my education. The storm of self-condemnation raged because I felt I had betrayed their trust and squandered their sacrifices.

This cloud made me wonder if they would love me again. That fear, the existential terror of being cut off from my primary source of unconditional support, was far worse than any physical pain. I felt I had forfeited my place in their hearts, that the daughter they loved, the one who fought so hard to succeed, was now overshadowed by the one who had made the mistake.

My first action, born of the deepest desperation, was a reflex. Before I could move, speak, or plan, I first asked God, Please forgive me for making the decision I did. This was not a prayer of convenience; it was a primal, gut-wrenching cry of surrender. I knew I couldn't fix this myself, and I knew that if human love failed me, divine love was the only thing that could keep me whole. I confessed the wrong choice and immediately sought the one, constant, unshakable source of grace. This act, rooted in the foundational faith I had been taught, was the first step toward bouncing forward from a self-inflicted wound.

Grace in the Storm

The storm reached its zenith when I could no longer hide the truth. In the rush of labor, the hospital got in touch with my parents to tell them what was going on and where I was.

At that time, I felt like the storm had become too much for me to bear. Lying in that sterile hospital bed, so far from home (they had to come all the way from Mansfield, Louisiana, to Ruston, Louisiana, a journey of over a hundred miles), I was utterly alone and physically spent. I laid in bed praying that the storm would calm down. I was not asking for the consequence to disappear; I was asking for the *strength* to face it. I asked Him to help me bear whatever I had to endure. I was seeking that supernatural strength I had found years earlier in the kitchen, the strength that was not my own.

Then came the miracle of love.

My mother made it to the hospital. Though the journey was over a hundred miles and on unfamiliar roads, it seemed like it had only been a few seconds that had passed when she arrived. The nurse brought her to my room.

The sight of her face, weary from the journey but shining with a mixture of fear, disappointment, and incandescent love, broke the dam of my carefully constructed control. In that moment, the floodgates opened. I was crying; a deep, cleansing, desperate, racking cry that released months of guilt and fear. And she was praying.

She didn't lecture me. She didn't condemn me. Even in her disappointments, she showed love to my baby and me. Her presence was the anchor dropped into the deepest, darkest water of my soul. I watched her, this woman who had taught me the meaning of endurance, kneel by my bed and pray not just for me, but for the tiny new life that had just entered the world.

That was a huge relief from the storm. The true terror was not the physical childbirth; it was the fear of rejection. When she showed up, praying and loving, the central fear was neutralized. She was there for me and my baby boy.

We talked, and in that moment of profound vulnerability, she gave him a name that carried the weight of destiny, a name that signified strength, faith, and the promise of a future: David. I proudly added Jerome Brooks, a name to mark his lineage. Lying there, gazing at my son and feeling my mother's hand on my forehead, I knew the storm hadn't destroyed me; it had merely forced me into the shelter of grace.

I had made a wrong turn, but God, through the tangible, sacrificial love of my mother, had carried me back to the right road.

The Cold Front at Home

The physical recovery began quickly, but the emotional reckoning was waiting for me back at the farm. We went home, and another storm rose up unexpectedly. This one was a cold front, silent and heavy, and it centered on my father.

This was the time I had to depend wholly on my foundation of Faith for this one, because the silence of a disappointed parent can be louder and more damaging than any shouting match. My father was not as loving as my mother. He wouldn't come around us, and he wouldn't speak to me. His disappointment was a palpable, chilling presence in the house, a constant reminder that I had failed the standard he had worked so hard to establish.

I felt God's presence immediately, powerfully, and unequivocally all around me and my son. The Lord knew I couldn't face this silent rejection alone. In those first few weeks, I spent hours rocking David, praying silently, asking for my father's heart to be softened. The spiritual warfare was subtle: fighting the urge to retreat into self-pity and instead choosing to remain open to reconciliation.

It was my mother, the constant source of practical spiritual wisdom, who ultimately gave me the courage to stay the course. I could hear her voice, firm and loving, in my ear: "*Your blood is in that room. So, you need to pray and get it together because they are here now and they are not going anywhere.*"

Her counsel was a profound theological lesson disguised as a parental lecture. It was a reminder that the bond of family is a covenant, not a contract, conditional on performance. David was here. He was *family*. I had to accept the consequence, stand my ground, and wait for the natural law of love to win out. The storm would pass, but only if I remained anchored in prayer.

The Dawning of Reconciliation

I took my mother's words to heart. I continued to pray, I continued to show up, and I continued to do my best to manage my new life with David, all while enduring my father's silent, heavy disapproval. It took time; days that felt like weeks, but gradually, the dam began to crack.

Then, one afternoon, I saw it.

He started coming around. Tentatively at first, a quick glance into the room, a brief inquiry about the baby's needs. Then, one day, he approached the crib. I watched, holding my breath, as the big, calloused hands that had coaxed life from the soil reached out and gently touched the tiny fingers of his grandson.

And then, he started playing with my son.

The moment I saw my farmer father, the unyielding man of the earth, break into a rare, gentle smile as he played with David Jerome Brooks, I felt an internal shift more significant than any tectonic plate movement. The sun began to shine. The storm didn't just calm down; it dissipated entirely, replaced by the warmth of acceptance and the quiet joy of a grandfather's love. My mistake had not destroyed the family; it had, in a strange, profound way, expanded it. I had *bounced forward* into a more complex, deeper, and more gracious relationship with the man I loved and feared most.

The Final Farewell

In the midst of this beautiful new chapter, a transition occurred that brought a quiet sense of closure to the foundational era of my life. My grandmother was living with us in the home. She was a constant, comforting presence, a living link to the past, and she had taken great joy in the arrival of her great-grandson.

She enjoyed playing with my son immensely, her love a gentle, unconditional balm to the house. I remember watching her, her old hands so fragile yet so capable of giving comfort, as she held David. It was as if she were blessing his entry into this difficult world, passing on the quiet dignity and enduring faith that had sustained our family for generations.

Shortly after that, she passed away in May the following year.

Her passing was not a Category 5 disaster; it was a quiet transition, a gentle rain after a long period of storm. Because of the deep, recent experience of God's constant presence, this loss, while profoundly sad, did not shake my foundation. It was a natural conclusion to a beautiful life, and the fact that she had lived to meet and hold David felt like a final, loving gift to me. Her life and her death, coming so close to the reconciliation with my father, felt like the final, definitive end of the foundation storms of my youth.

The woman who emerged from this crucible, college interrupted, a single mother, tested by fear and disappointment, was immeasurably stronger. I had made a grievous mistake, but God had not only forgiven it; He had woven it into the tapestry of my purpose. The scars were present, but they now carried the evidence of grace, not just grit. I was ready for the next season, equipped not just with tenacity but with the undeniable, living testament that no matter how hard the storm blows, you are never alone. The greater, more complicated storms were still ahead, but now I knew the secret: how to be carried.

PART TWO

THE STORMS OF LOSS

Chapter 3

The Loss of My Son

The woman who had just navigated the treacherous waters of shame and unexpected motherhood had, by the end of that turbulent year, convinced herself she was untouchable. The birth of my son, David Jerome Brooks, had been the storm of my own making, yet I was miraculously sheltered by the grace of my mother and the slow-dawning love of my father. I had proven that even from a self-inflicted wound, it was possible to bounce forward. I was a college-bound mother, equipped with grit, adaptability, and a profound, living faith.

The foundation, I believed, was set. The house was finally ready for a gentle, steady sail. I had earned the calm.

But life, as I had repeatedly learned, offers no guarantee of calm. The storms of my past had been external trials: a fire, a debilitating accident, a relocation, social exclusion, and even the self-inflicted wound of an early pregnancy. Each of those storms had challenged the structure, but never the cornerstone of my identity. The next season of my life, the brief, beautiful, and devastating eighteen months that followed my son's birth, would put every lesson I had ever learned, every whisper of faith, into a terrifying, ultimate action. This time, the storm would not just threaten the house; it would threaten the foundation of the earth beneath my feet.

The storm that was coming was the kind that broke the sky.

When Everything Changed

My son was one year and seven months old. His name, David Jerome Brooks, echoed through the house, a mixture of biblical strength and family lineage. He was more than a child; he was the sunshine after the thunder, the living proof of my redemption. He was the reason my farmer-father, the man whose approval I feared most, had learned to smile again. The house, which had once felt heavy with the silence of my father's disappointment, was now filled with the joyful sound of David's small, purposeful movements, his sudden, delightful laughter, and the simple, perfect warmth of a life that was finally on the right, difficult-but-blessed path. I had returned to my studies, carrying the title of mother and student with fierce, tenacious pride.

Then came the first, subtle shift in the atmospheric pressure. A high fever.

It was the quietest start to the most violent storm. It was not a sudden burst of flame or the clamor of a broken world; it was the silent, unnerving heat radiating from a child who was normally so vibrant. His energy, usually an insistent, demanding force, receded. He was listless, his eyes glazed with a dull sheen I didn't recognize. The mother in me, already hardened by the lessons of my own youth, knew immediately that this was not a simple, passing ailment. This was the first cold wind of a major system moving in. The instincts honed from years of diagnosing a sick calf or spotting a change in the cotton crop now screamed a warning far more terrifying than any natural phenomenon.

We packed quickly, propelled by a primal fear. The familiar hundred-mile journey from the quiet of Mansfield, Louisiana, to the emergency room in Ruston was a blur of mounting dread. My mother was with me, her presence a silent, desperate prayer. The journey was not just geographical; it was an emotional passage from the world of a high-achieving college student and new mother back into the vulnerable, terrifying space of a child facing overwhelming forces.

Behind the Closed Door

The moment we arrived, the wind picked up speed. The hospital, usually a place of sterile calm, felt like a vortex of activity centered entirely around my tiny son.

The staff, a blur of nurses and doctors in blue and white, moved with a frantic, purposeful speed that stripped away any remaining pretense of routine. They spoke in clipped, technical language that served only to underscore the gravity of the situation. *Meningitis.* The word was whispered and then repeated, and it sounded like the grinding of tectonic plates, a force far beyond human control.

They took my son into an examining room, and in one of the most agonizing moments of my life, we were not allowed in the room with him.

I was separated from the one life I was pledged to protect. I was forced to be an observer in the waiting area while the battle for my son's life was fought just feet away, behind a closed, swinging door. The air in the waiting room became thick and heavy, like the humidity before a devastating summer squall. This was the true, initial force of the wind, the feeling of utter helplessness. I was a woman of action, of grit, of endurance, but I could do nothing but wait. The lessons of agency and control, so painstakingly learned, were rendered meaningless.

The updates were sparse, brief moments of human contact in the growing maelstrom. Every ten or fifteen minutes, a doctor or nurse would emerge, their faces grave, and offer a short sentence or two about fluid retention, spinal tap results, or declining vitals, before vanishing back behind the closed door. Each word, each shake of a doctor's head, was a fresh clap of thunder directly over my head. My mother and I were locked in a cycle of praying and crying. The structured faith that had guided me through high school and college was now being tested in its rawest, most elemental form, reduced to guttural cries and whispered, repetitive pleas.

When the Ground Gave Way

The emotional pressure was physical. I couldn't sit still. The anxiety was a hurricane inside my body, the high winds of the storm vibrating through my nerves. I paced the narrow confines of the waiting area, tracing the same worn path on the tiled floor. My hands were balled into fists, and I was shaking out of control. My body was reacting to the spiritual truth of the moment: the ground was becoming unsteady. I was losing my footing. I was falling to my knees.

In those endless minutes, I whispered the prayer that had been my anchor through the fire and the pregnancy: *"God, carry me."* But this time, I was not asking for strength to face the pain; I was asking for the will to survive the inevitable. I was begging for a lifeline before the inevitable, terrifying wave crashed. My mind flashed back to the Fire Pit Accident, the initial injury, the physical pain, but this was a thousand times worse. That was my body; this was my heart, my future, the living testament to my hard-won redemption.

The waiting ended with the arrival of the lead physician.

He didn't stand over me, looming in authority. He came and knelt down beside me, bringing his eyes level with mine as I sat, hunched and shaking, on the hard, plastic chair. In the clinical, polished environment of the hospital, this simple, humble act carried the weight of a final, terrible pronouncement. His eyes were not cold or professional; they were heavy with shared grief, a profound human sadness that transcended his role.

He spoke the words that became the lightning strike of my life: *"We have done everything we could to save your son."*

The Storm That Broke the Sky

The thunder that followed was not an external sound; it was the shattering of the internal sky. It was the sound of a carefully built future collapsing into a vacuum. I lost it. The control that had been my hallmark, the quiet self-reserve of the farm girl, the tenacity of the student, snapped.

This was the storm that broke the sky. This was the Category 5 hurricane I had always been preparing for, but never truly believed would arrive. The earlier trials, the physical pain, the academic struggle, the social exclusion, even the pregnancy, were foundational skirmishes. This was the greatest, most complicated Life Storm I had yet to face. It came full force, and I had no idea how I would survive it. The wind was blowing, the thunder was rolling, and the lightning was flashing until I fell to my knees, utterly unable to support my own weight. I was a child again, completely exposed and defenseless.

In that moment of absolute, elemental loss, the world rushed in with a strange, cushioning force. People in the waiting room came to console us, and they were crying, too. These were strangers, people waiting for their own medical outcomes, yet they were swept up in the immediate, universal agony of a mother's loss. Even the hospital staff, hardened to the realities of life and death, gathered around us, expressing how sorry they were for our loss.

This outpouring of shared human grief was a strange, unexpected current of support in the middle of the storm's eye. It was the first soft evidence of the carrying to come.

In that instant, with my world shattered and my physical body incapable of movement, I had to make the most crucial decision of my life: I realized that I had to depend on the foundation I had in God. It was not a choice of convenience; it was a reflex of survival, an automatic turn to the only source of absolute constancy I had ever known. The same foundational faith that had been tested and refined was now the only anchor left in the raging waters.

And then, the miracle of the carrying began.

Immediately, I could feel God's presence all around me. It was not a physical warmth, but a powerful, supernatural peace that descended into the conflicts of my soul. It was a tangible cessation of the internal storm, even as the external reality remained horrific. I could almost hear Him talking to me, not in audible words, but in the certainty of a presence that was absolute and unwavering: *I am here. You will not drown.* He was carrying me in this weakest moment. The outpouring support from strangers and staff, which was an earthly manifestation of grace, became a tangible force that lifted the storm off my chest and gave me the inexplicable strength to simply breathe; to accept the reality that my son had died from an acute case of meningitis.

The greatest blow had been delivered, and yet, I was still standing, or rather, I was being held upright.

The Cold Reality and a Gift of Grace

The storm did not dissipate. After the lightning strike of the news, the cold, logistical front of grief rolled in. The body, the spirit, the mind, all must engage in the grim reality of a final farewell. It was time to make preparations for my son to be buried, and the wind began blowing again, a chilling, hollow, purposeful wind that drove us into the next agonizing task.

Our first, most heartbreaking task was to buy the clothes. To walk into a store, searching for an outfit that would dress a child for eternity, was a profound, surreal kind of pain. It felt like a perverse act of preparation, a denial of all the forward motion I had fought for.

We went inside the store, the fluorescent lights harsh and unforgiving against the backdrop of our fresh, debilitating grief. The store manager approached us, asking if he could help us find anything. He took one look at us, at the grief etched on our faces, the red-rimmed eyes, the silent desperation, and then he recognized my parents, the people of the land, the pillars of the community. He saw the purpose in our hands, searching through tiny garments.

He saw, and he understood.

"My God, your baby!" he exclaimed. The grief in his voice was raw and immediate.

He stopped, his professional demeanor falling away, replaced by an authentic, gut-level compassion. He made an immediate, profound gesture: *"Don't worry about buying anything,"* he told us. *"I'm going to take care of this expense for you."*

The shock of his kindness was another type of emotional deluge. This was grace manifested as a debt canceled. The flood waters started again as the pressure of that specific task was suddenly released. This man, who knew my parents very well, was offering not just a financial reprieve, but a moment of unearned human grace in a time of utter desperation. He was an instrument of the carrying.

He recognized my state of shock and fragility. He sat me down with a glass of water so I could compose myself. He was a quiet, practical shepherd in the midst of my emotional wilderness, making sure I had the physical strength to endure the next step.

Then, he delivered the divine whisper that would become my future directive. He turned to me, gave me a hug, and said, *"I want you to go back to school and let it be in remembrance of your son."*

This was not a suggestion; it was a command wrapped in a blessing. It was a challenge to reclaim the identity I had worked so hard to build, a sacred task to turn my grief into purpose. He was giving David's life and death a meaning that transcended the pain. He made sure I was composed enough to go out of the store and told me to try not to talk to anyone outside because I was too weak to speak. He protected me from the inevitable, sympathetic questions that would have broken my fragile composure. He gave us the clothes, and we left, carrying the clothes and the incredible weight of his kindness, thanking him for his profound generosity.

The Downpour at the Funeral Home

We then headed to the funeral home. The short trip was a fresh wave of the storm, one that dissolved the brief shelter of the store. The wind started blowing again, I heard the thunder rolling and lightning flashing, and the flooding had washed away my taught of mind by then. The cumulative trauma was dissolving my capacity for rational thought. The reality of the ultimate finality was upon us.

After that round of thunder, lightning, and flooding, we faced the next agonizing task: making the selection for the casket to put him in. To look at the symbols of finality for a life that was just beginning was a downpour too heavy to bear. It was a moment of choosing the final bed for my child. It was such a downpour of thunder, lightning, and flooding that I had to lean on my mother's shoulder before I could move and get some relief. My mother, the constant anchor, was the physical manifestation of the carrying, my rock against the gale of sorrow.

The funeral director, a man whose life was spent in the constant shadow of grief, offered another surprising moment of shelter.

He had a prayer with us. He told us simply to *"just trust God, and He will make things better."* It was not a trite saying; it was a professional's declaration of faith, a spiritual directive in a secular setting.

He looked at us, his eyes conveying a special kind of respect, and said, *"This is my job, and I have seen many families come through that door, but it's something special about you all."* He paused, a moment of profound vulnerability, and added, *"Maybe it's because I never lost a child, but we are going to make it."* He saw the fragility of our foundation, but saw the strength of the faith holding us together.

He then gave us a directive of grace: *"Now I want you all to go home,"* he said, and he would have my son ready for viewing the next

41

day. He gave us permission to rest, to retreat from the storm's immediate demands, a space of grace before the final act.

The Long Night of Dread

We went home and waited. The storm had not passed, but the intensity had shifted. The wind was blowing, but God gave me the strength to endure it much better. The active, visceral pain had settled into a heavy, sleepless dread.

All night, I was not able to get much sleep. My mind was consumed with one thought: What would my son look like? The next day, we had to go and approve my son for public viewing. It was the last act of a mother, and the pressure was immense; a final, terrifying moment of judgment on the presentation of my child.

It was a difficult process, but with my Faith and trust in God, the storm felt lighter. The constant presence of the divine, the same presence that had filled the waiting room and the funeral home, was now filling the void in my own room. He carried me all the way through this storm of grief, and He carried me every step of the way. I could feel His strength in this storm filled with high winds, thunder, lightning, and flooding. The carrying was not an absence of the storm, but a supernatural endurance within it. The funeral was held, a blur of sorrow and community support, and David Jerome Brooks was laid to rest.

After the funeral, the immediate rush of logistical and social activity ceased. The shared grief receded, and I was left alone with the wreckage. The wind, thunder, and lightning were gone, replaced by a cold, unrelenting front of depression.

I didn't know what to do or how to keep living without my son. The loss was a vacuum, a terrifying silence where a vibrant life had been. My carefully constructed identity, the student, the mother, the survivor, had been completely destabilized. I retreated into myself, unable to reconcile the depth of my grief with the necessity of survival. I felt the familiar pull of self-pity and spiritual isolation.

Once again, the woman who had taught me the meaning of endurance became my shelter. It was my mother praying and talking to me, and God carrying me, that allowed me to eventually get through it. She was the steady human voice guiding me back to the divine anchor, refusing to let me sink into the quiet depths of despair.

Slowly, tentatively, I started the climb back. I started talking and going back to church. The return to the community of faith was a deliberate step toward reclamation. For it was the realization that my foundation and Faith would carry me all the way that became my guiding light. With that assurance, the sun could shine again in my life.

The Memory That Moves Me Forward

It was time for summer school. The store manager's challenge, "go back to school in remembrance of your son," was now a concrete, terrifying opportunity. It was the only way forward, the only way to transform the pain into purpose.

My mother, with her practical, spiritual wisdom, encouraged me to go back to school for the summer. She gave me the gift of conditional permission: she told me that if it was stressful and I could not manage it, then we would do something else later. This release from the pressure of absolute success was the final push I needed. I didn't have to conquer the world; I just had to try to take the first step.

I did as my mother requested. It was difficult at times, the grief a constant, heavy presence, but I had some carrying roommates, other human manifestations of God's grace, and that helped me manage and get through the storm. The sheer grit that had been forged in the cotton fields was now applied to the crucible of grief. Each day, the wind blew lighter, and I was able to live through the storm better.

My son's death was the ultimate test. It had pushed me beyond the limits of my own grit and into the center of a profound, life-altering truth: **no matter how hard the storm blows, the only way to survive is to be carried.** It will always be a memory that I can't forget, but it is a memory now surrounded by the evidence of a boundless, life-sustaining grace. The woman who had emerged from the hospital with a baby and a renewed sense of purpose had been broken and remade in the wake of his death. My scars now carried the evidence of a profound truth: I knew how to stand, and more importantly, I knew how to *be carried* when standing was no longer possible.

Chapter 4

The Storm of Identity

Finding Purpose After Loss

The funeral of my son, David Jerome Brooks, marked not just the end of a life, but the abrupt, violent close of one entire chapter of my own. I had weathered the storm of an early, unexpected pregnancy, survived the crushing grief of a fire, and even endured the shame of social exclusion. But the loss of David, the living proof of my hard-won redemption, was an elemental event. It was the moment the earth itself shifted, and I was left standing on ground that no longer felt solid. Yet, God had carried me through that initial, blinding deluge of pain. The sheer, terrifying vulnerability of that moment, the realization that my own grit and tenacity were utterly insufficient, had forced a complete surrender to grace.

Now, as the immediate, visible storm of grief receded, another, more insidious challenge emerged: the storm of identity. I was no longer the college-bound mother under the vigilant, protective watch of my parents. I was an adult, a survivor of ultimate loss, standing at the edge of the world and realizing that the wind that blew toward me now was my own. It was a wind that demanded self-sufficiency, direction, and a new kind of faith, one that navigated the terrifying unknown without the physical presence of my lifelong anchors.

The familiar, quiet life on the farm, surrounded by my parents' towering strength, had always been a shelter. Even my schooling had been a controlled environment, a path dictated by established curriculum and familial expectation. But adulthood was an immense, frightening ocean. There was no syllabus, no blueprint, and no guaranteed path to success. The safety net of parental protection, while still spiritually present, was geographically and practically pulled back. I had to learn to follow the way without their direct help, relying entirely on the lessons of faith and the innate grit they had instilled.

The sheer volume of decisions facing me became a source of internal panic. Every morning was a confrontation with the void: What career? Where to live? How to manage the hollow space left by David's absence? The storm of *doubt* appeared not as a single flash of lightning, but as a persistent, gray drizzle, questioning every move, every choice. The unknown was not just frightening; it was truly terrifying. My mind, usually focused and tenacious, wrestled with the anxiety of making a wrong decision. A wrong decision now felt like it could lead to ruin, especially with the financial responsibilities that loomed without the anchor of a stable, long-term career.

My primary focus became translating the grit of farming, the knowledge that persistence and planning yield a harvest, into the foreign terrain of the corporate world. The farmer's life is one of constant, tangible struggle: you see the field, you feel the dirt, you measure the rain. Adulthood and career hunting felt like trying to plant seeds in the darkness. The realization that life as an adult meant thinking straight, making rational, long-term decisions that affected not just myself but my future, became the main goal. It was the ultimate test of my maturity, and it was a test I could not afford to fail.

The early attempts at defining my path were marked by a desperate prayer for God's direction. I knew that if I stepped out in my own limited strength, I would be swept away. The career search became a spiritual quest: What was the purpose of this life that had been so dramatically remade through fire and grief? I prayed for a sign, a clear direction from the wind. I needed an opportunity that felt less like a job and more like a calling, something stable and reliable that could rebuild the security shattered by the storm of loss.

The Pursuit of a Career

The answer came not as a spiritual whisper in a quiet church, but as a loud, material announcement in the local community: *Western Electric* was coming to Shreveport, Louisiana.

This was a massive, new industrial plant, a beacon of stability and the promise of a long-term, successful career. For our area, a new manufacturing plant was nothing short of a divine economic intervention. The news, buzzing through the community, felt like the first shift in the wind after a long, devastating period of stillness. I was still a college student, trying to navigate the summer semester my mother and the store manager had encouraged me to take in David's memory. Yet, the gravitational pull of guaranteed employment and financial independence was too strong to ignore.

When the semester ended, I felt an almost magnetic compulsion to apply. The trip to the Western Electric facility felt like a pilgrimage. I remember the building towering, massive, and impersonal, a complete contrast to the open fields of the cotton farm, yet offering a promise of a different kind of harvest, the reliable paycheck, the benefits, the security. The sheer size of the operation, the endless lines of vehicles, and the stream of hopeful applicants made the endeavor feel daunting, but the farmer's resolve, the understanding that you simply show up and do the work, propelled me forward.

I applied for a summer job, expecting a bureaucratic tangle of forms and waiting lists. Instead, I was swept into a rapid-fire sequence of interviews and standardized tests. The process was cold, analytical, and technical, measuring aptitude rather than personality or background. I moved from room to room, feeling the pressure build. Each test presented a new hurdle: mechanical comprehension, spatial reasoning, and mathematical aptitude. I drew upon the intense focus cultivated during my college studies and the deep concentration required to manage the emotional turmoil of the past year.

In what felt like a moment of miraculous sunshine, I was hired on the spot. I passed every single test, achieving scores that impressed the hiring manager. The ease of this success, following years of struggle, felt astonishing. It was as if God had simply cleared the path. I had prayed for direction, and He had provided an open door that no human gatekeeper could shut. The offer of immediate, stable employment was a powerful antidote to the fear and financial anxiety that had been the background noise of my life since David's passing. I accepted the job immediately, putting my college education on hold. The logic was simple: a guaranteed, successful career was the foundation I needed, and the time for academic pursuits could wait. I had found the path, and it was shining brightly. I had convinced myself this was the right choice, the wind was blowing in my direction, leading me to a prosperous and secure future.

The thirteen years I spent at Western Electric were defined by a profound sense of stability and hard work. The initial sun that shone so brightly on my career choice never seemed to dim. The work was demanding, often repetitive, but it offered the structured, measurable success that my farmer's soul appreciated. I exchanged the unpredictable chaos of the weather and the earth for the predictable rhythm of the assembly line and the guaranteed weekly wage. It was a life built on solid, material ground, and it allowed me to finally stop shaking and start rebuilding.

I became a master of my station, a diligent and reliable employee. The stability of the job provided the emotional distance I needed from the raw pain of losing David. The routine, the clocking in, the focused labor, the clocking out, was a comforting shield. I channeled all the energy that had once been consumed by grief and academic ambition into making a successful life.

This stability was the great shelter I had built after the great storm. It provided a financial anchor, a respected place in the community, and the feeling that I was finally in control of my destiny again. I learned the language of the plant, the dynamics of the factory floor, and the technical specifics of my job with unwavering focus. The security was intoxicating. It was easy to believe that I had engineered my way out of the storm entirely, using my own tenacity and the opportunities God had placed before me. It felt like I had made it: a successful career choice, a solid future, a life finally free from the threat of ruin.

But the most dangerous storms are the ones that build silently beneath a bright sky.

The Storm of Destruction

Life is not a static calculation, and every self-made shelter is subject to tests it cannot foresee. After thirteen years of diligent service, during a routine but strenuous moment of my job, I felt a sharp, agonizing *snap* in my lower back. It was not the dramatic fall of the fire or the sudden, swift illness of David; it was a small, internal collapse, a betrayal by my own body that felt exponentially more terrifying because it happened in the very place, my secure career, I had built to protect myself.

The injury was debilitating. The subsequent diagnosis led to the inevitable, chilling pronouncement: back surgery.

The storm that followed was the storm of destruction because it didn't just injure me; it crushed the entire foundation of my life built around my career. Suddenly, the strength and stamina I had always relied on, the very physical capacity that defined my worth on the factory floor, were gone.

The post-surgical recovery period was a profound form of spiritual exile. I was forced into stillness, a kind of suspended animation that contrasted violently with my nature as a person of action, work, and forward motion. The pain was physical, but the true agony was existential. I was dependent on doctors, on medications, on my family for day-to-day living. My financial security, which I had

49

considered ironclad, now rested precariously on disability payments and the uncertain promise of re-employment.

The wind and rain increased during this time of recovery. Every day was a confrontation with the unknown. Would I ever fully recover? Could I physically return to the only career I had known for over a decade? I lay in bed, the silence of my recovery broken only by the flood of anxious thoughts: *Did I make the right career choice thirteen years ago? What if I can no longer work? Who am I without my ability to provide?*

I had to make many adjustments to my living. I was forced to look at my budget, cancel non-essential expenses, and rely on the kindness and patience of others, something a fiercely independent farm girl finds agonizing. The uncertainty, the pressure on my living situation, and the sheer volume of time spent in reflection all served to deepen my dependence on God's direction. The physical weakness was a spiritual strength training; it stripped away the illusion of self-control and forced me back to the foundational truth: the only way to survive is to be carried.

Finally, after months of painful recovery and rehabilitation, my doctor released me for light duty. I felt a wave of relief so intense it was almost dizzying. This was it, the return, the proof that the storm had passed, and I could reclaim my life.

I returned to Western Electric, buoyed by the prospect of rejoining my colleagues and getting back to work. I had followed the medical protocols, endured the surgery, and healed. I was ready to contribute again.

But a new, unexpected storm came up quickly, catching me completely by surprise. I had overlooked a critical, institutional hurdle: I had to be cleared by the plant's medical department.

When I arrived at the plant, the atmosphere was thick with unspoken tension. I was directed to the medical office, a small, clinical space within the massive facility, a place I had only ever visited for minor cuts or mandatory annual checks. As I waited in the small, fluorescent-lit waiting area, the sense of dread was palpable. I saw the lightning flashing in my mind and heard the thunder rolling. I was shaking from the unknown, the sudden, sharp realization that the administrative wing of the company held all the power over my future, not my own doctor's release.

When they called me to the examining room, I expected a routine review of my personal physician's release form. I expected them to confirm the light-duty limitations and assign me a temporary desk job. The company doctor and the human resources representative sat across the sterile metal desk. Their faces were kind, professional, and utterly devoid of warmth.

The doctor spoke, and his words were the single, massive clap of thunder that broke the entire sky a second time:

"Due to the severity of your surgery, we don't have any position that you could do, even on light duty, that would not risk further injury to your back. We have to consider the long-term liability."

The word "liability" echoed in the small room. It was cold, corporate, and absolute.

At that moment, the sky truly burst. I was hit with the storm of acceptance; acceptance that the career I had spent thirteen years building, the security I had fought for after the grief of losing David, the whole physical and financial structure of my life, was now destroyed.

I was drowning in the floodwaters of disappointment. The sense of betrayal was overwhelming. Thirteen years of loyalty and hard work had been erased by a single cold, professional assessment. I felt a dizzying pressure, a vacuum of purpose. What was I supposed to do now? The future I had envisioned was gone, replaced by an abyss of unemployment and financial fear. The shame of returning to my parents, of being unable to care for myself, of being fundamentally *broken* by my own body, was immense. The wind was howling, and I was alone on the wreckage.

Unemployment and Unshakable Faith

Because I was no longer able to work, my financial situation became a grave, immediate problem. Paying my bills morphed from a predictable routine into a daily, gut-wrenching struggle. The pressure on my living situation was extreme, driving me back to the only source I knew to be constant.

This was the moment the rising of my religious Faith stepped in, not as a comfort, but as an absolute necessity. The emotional space left vacant by the loss of my career was immediately filled by the presence of God's direction. I knew, without a shadow of a doubt, that I could not navigate this complex, bureaucratic, and terrifying storm on my own.

I turned constantly to the word of God. The Scripture that became my anchor during this period of intense weakness and uncertainty was **2 Corinthians 12:9-10 (King James Version of the Bible)**:

"And he said unto me, My grace is sufficient for thee: for my strength is made perfect in weakness. Most gladly, therefore, will I rather glory in my infirmities, that the power of Christ may rest upon me. Therefore, I take pleasure in infirmities, in reproaches, in necessities, in persecutions, in distresses for Christ's sake: for when I am weak, then am I strong."

This passage was a life raft. The world had told me I was weak and a liability. The Lord reminded me that my weakness was the very prerequisite for His strength. This realization gave me the internal fortitude to withstand the storm. The external conditions, the lack of work, the financial strain, were still pressing, but the inner pressure, the fear of complete ruin, was lifted.

After letting God lead and guide me through the complicated process of paperwork and waiting, I was able to draw unemployment benefits. It was a temporary reprieve, a floatation device tossed to me in the floodwaters, and it allowed me to endure the storm much better. The wind was still blowing, and the financial reality was still grim, but I could breathe. I understood that unemployment was only temporary, a bridge, not a destination. I was still praying fervently for an opportunity to find stable employment that matched my new physical limitations. The clouds were still forming at times, threatening to obscure my hope, but God would let the sun shine every now and then, providing just enough light to keep me moving forward. The faith that had been forged in the crucible of David's loss was now fully operational, directing my every step. I was learning to be carried even when the ground was missing entirely.

A Phone Call from DeSoto Parish

The period of waiting and uncertainty felt endless, but the moment of rescue arrived with the deceptive quietness of a simple phone call. I was sitting in my den, the atmosphere heavy with the weight of my unemployed status, when the phone rang.

The very sound was startling. Why would anyone be calling me? What could it be? The uncertainty was immediate. Was this another test, another bureaucratic hurdle, or, finally, a sign of hope? Little did I know, the clouds were moving, and the sun was about to shine for me again.

I answered the phone, and on the other end was the principal of an elementary school in DeSoto Parish. At the time, I was known as Mrs. Richardson.

She didn't waste time on formalities. She simply asked, "Can you come to the school?"

I replied immediately, "Yes, ma'am, I will be right there."

This was the cloud of not knowing. The question hung in the air: Why was she calling? Why did she want to see *me*? I was dressed quickly, propelled by a mixture of anxiety and an inexplicable surge of hope.

When I arrived, she carried me into her office; a deliberate, welcoming act that contrasted so sharply with the cold, impersonal dismissal I had received at the medical office. She asked me to sit down. The small act of sitting, of being welcomed and treated with dignity, was a balm to my shattered self-esteem.

She began to speak, and her words were like the sun breaking through the storm clouds.

She said that she had heard about my situation: the injury, the surgery, the unexpected loss of my job. The community knowledge, which had once felt like a source of intrusive pressure, was now the source of grace. She knew I had left college to go to work at Western Electric, and she delivered the incredible news: I had enough college hours to work within the education system.

The sun started shining bright again in my life. The pieces of my abandoned college journey, the credits I had accumulated with such fierce effort, were suddenly a currency for a new life. This was the divine economy: nothing was wasted. The path I had abandoned for the promise of factory wages was now the very thing saving me from the abyss of unemployment.

She initially wanted me to work in the office. However, office work felt too constrained, too bureaucratic. I was not comfortable working in that position. I needed a role where I could interact, contribute, and truly *work* with a sense of mission. I chose a position that spoke to my need for purpose and service: working in the Lab.

This Lab was a specialized resource for students who did not score high enough on the *California Achievement Test (CAT)*. These were the students who needed extra guidance, patience, and a dedicated, focused mentor to help them catch up.

The choice of the Lab was immediate and intuitive. It was a role that demanded the same resilience, focus, and tenacious belief in a slow, difficult harvest that my father had taught me on the farm. But more than that, it was an opportunity to pour my energy, which had been so bitterly consumed by loss and struggle, into the lives of vulnerable children. It was a complete reversal of the physical damage: my back was broken, but my mind and spirit were now fully engaged in the work of restoration.

The sun started shining bright again. I had found employment, and more importantly, I had found a vocation.

One more time, **God carried me,** and I was able to rise from that storm. The journey through the storm of identity, the initial career security, the bodily betrayal, the professional rejection, and the financial hardship had all been necessary steps. They stripped away my reliance on material success and physical strength, leaving only the bedrock of my faith. My unexpected job loss was not destruction; it was a divine redirection, opening the door to a career that offered not just a paycheck, but a profound opportunity to serve and heal.

I realized that the greatest storms are never just about endurance; they are always about the inevitable *carrying* that brings you to a brighter, more purposeful shore. The storm had ended, and I was back on my feet, ready to face the long, rewarding work of a new life. The sun, finally, was shining brightly. The storm had broken the sky so that a new, clear vision could emerge. I was no longer defined by what I had lost or what I could no longer do, but by the quiet, powerful strength of what I was being called to become. This was the true beginning of my life as an adult, one anchored not in the soil, but in the spirit.

The Harvest of the Spirit

The transition from the noisy, industrial rhythm of the plant to the vibrant, yet often chaotic, environment of the elementary school Lab was a complete emotional and sensory shock. In the factory, success was measured in units produced and defects avoided; it was cold, quantitative, and absolute. In the Lab, success was measured in incremental gains on a young student's comprehension, in the spark of understanding in a child's eye, and in the building of confidence; it was qualitative, messy, and infinitely rewarding.

The physical environment was a world away from the factory floor. The plant was vast, deafening, and driven by the relentless ticking of the clock, demanding perfect synchronization from human hands and automated machinery. The Lab was a small, contained space, painted in cheerful colors, filled with the scent of paper, crayons, and the quiet hum of concentration. Instead of the loud clanging of tools, I heard the rustle of turning pages, the soft scratch of pencils, and the hesitant whispers of children struggling with a concept. The chaos here was the chaos of potential, untapped brilliance waiting for the right key to unlock it.

My first few weeks were a steep learning curve. The industrial mindset had to be completely purged. I was used to giving an instruction and seeing an immediate, measurable output. Here, I could give the same instruction five times, using five different methods, and still be met with a blank stare. Patience, which I thought I possessed in spades from years of waiting for the cotton crop to mature, had to be redefined. This was not the patience of the seasons; it was the patience of the spirit, the unhurried grace required to meet a struggling child exactly where they were.

The students were not simply test scores; they were individuals carrying their own burdens. There was the withdrawn student, whose head was always down, whose inability to read a passage was less about comprehension and more about the fear of public failure. There was the frustrated student, whose energy, much like my own in my factory days, was aggressive and defensive, translating academic difficulty into behavioral outbursts. I saw myself in their struggles: the fear of being deemed deficient, the deep shame of not meeting an imposed standard.

I approached my new role with the same farmer's grit that had defined my life. A struggling field needs soil amendments and targeted care; a struggling child needed targeted lessons and emotional nourishment. I learned to analyze their errors not as failures, but as diagnostic maps. A mistake was not a reason for punishment, but a signpost pointing exactly to the missing piece of the foundation.

This became the core of my new vocational philosophy. In the factory, I built circuit boards that had to be perfect. In the Lab, I was helping children build their own futures, and those futures were not defined by perfection but by resilience. Every time I witnessed a student's face light up with understanding, a small, private moment of revelation over a math problem or a difficult word, it felt like a more profound achievement than any quality control measure I had enforced on the assembly line. This was the harvest of the spirit, a new kind of yield that filled the vacuum left by my professional loss.

Scars and Sustenance

The external beauty of my new life, the sunshine of the Lab, was not an automatic cure for the deep physical and financial scars I carried. I was constantly reminded that I was not the same woman who had clocked in at Western Electric for thirteen years.

The back injury was a persistent, uninvited guest. The pain was no longer the acute agony of the initial injury or the immediate post-surgical period, but a chronic, low-level thrumming that dictated my movement. Teaching required constant, gentle adaptation. I could not stand for long periods. I could not bend or lift without careful planning. The simple, physical act of managing a classroom, bending down to a child's desk, moving stacks of books, became a conscious challenge, a daily reminder of the storm I had survived.

This physical limitation forced an extreme reliance on the *"light duty"* nature of my job, and more profoundly, on grace. I had to learn to ask for help, a devastating concept for a fiercely independent farm girl. I had to rely on the older, stronger students to help with tasks and on my colleagues to understand my physical boundaries. This dependency was humiliating at first, but it became the practical manifestation of my spiritual truth: when I was weak, He was strong. My back was broken, but it forced my pride to break too, making space for community and humility.

Financially, the transition was harsh. The teaching assistant salary, while a blessing and a lifeline, was significantly less than the factory wages I had earned. The financial recovery became a long, grinding journey of extreme frugality. The lingering anxiety over paying bills did not vanish; it became a low-grade fever I learned to live with. I budgeted meticulously, cutting costs to the bone. This period was not about abundance or rebuilding wealth; it was about staying afloat and surviving.

The experience cemented the true meaning of the word *sustenance*. It was the provision of just enough; enough income to cover the bills, enough strength to make it through the day, enough grace to handle the emotional demands of the children. It was a life lived hand-to-mouth with God, relying on His timely intervention rather than a massive savings account. The storm had taught me that I could lose everything, but the carrying meant that I would never be utterly abandoned. The teaching job was God's direct, practical answer to my prayer for employment, ensuring that my needs were met, even if my wants had to be permanently deferred.

Strength in Weakness

The most profound transformation occurred in the spiritual interpretation of my role. My core Scripture, **2 Corinthians 12:9-10**, was not just a comforting verse; it became a template for my curriculum in the Lab.

The text was a powerful counter-narrative to the message of the CAT test. The CAT test was a secular instrument of judgment; it identified weakness and labeled deficiency. But I knew that true strength began in the acknowledgment of weakness.

My mission, therefore, was to teach the children that their low scores were not permanent condemnations, but simply starting points. I taught them, through stories and parables, that a broken bone, once healed, is often stronger at the break point. The weakness identified by the test was the place where their true mental and spiritual strength could begin to grow.

I consciously transformed the Lab into a sanctuary of acceptance. I taught them that shame was a lie. Just as my job loss and subsequent dependency had been my pathway to relying on God's grace, their academic challenges were their opportunity to rely on the grace of the learning process. I shared my own story, without heavy detail, but with the undeniable sincerity of a survivor. I spoke of falling down and being carried, not by human strength, but by a Higher Power.

I translated the concept of *"God carried me"* into tangible classroom actions:

- **Patience as Grace:** When a student was exasperated, I would not rush them. I would sit beside them and repeat the lesson, viewing their slow uptake not as resistance, but as a plea for patience, the same patience God had shown me during my long, uncertain months of recovery.

- **Encouragement as Divine Direction:** I used specific, powerful words of affirmation. I told them they were smart, capable, and chosen. I was not complimenting their current skill level; I was declaring their potential, whispering God's truth into their young, discouraged spirits, just as the principal had whispered my new career into existence.
- **The Power of Humility:** I would openly admit when I didn't know the answer or when a concept was difficult for me to explain, demonstrating that vulnerability was a strength, not a weakness.

The Lab became my living, breathing testimony. The storm of identity that had begun with external trials, the loss of my son, the loss of my career, was finally resolved here. I realized my identity was not derived from my physical ability (factory worker) or my material success (income level), but from my absolute capacity to be a vessel for *God's carrying power*. My weakness became my qualification. My life's purpose was no longer an ambition I had to grit my teeth and force into existence, but a grace-filled path I was being led down.

The sun was shining brightly, not just for a moment, but as a settled, constant reality. The storm had broken the sky so that this new, clear vision could emerge. I was no longer defined by the wreckage of my past, but by the quiet, powerful strength of what I was being called to become, a woman who was strong because she was carried, and who now helped carry others. The foundation was set, not in the earth or in a paycheck, but in an enduring faith.

PART THREE

THE STORMS OF THE HEART

Chapter 5

The First Storm of the Heart,

(A Life Built on Shifting Sands)

Finding My Way Back to Love

The years after losing David, leaving Western Electric, and being called into the classroom brought a fragile but genuine peace. I had traded the steady paycheck of factory life for the steady purpose of teaching. The Academic Lab became my safe place, a space where I could guide others through their own storms and help them find strength on unsteady ground.

Yet outside that classroom, I was still a woman who longed for companionship. I had faith, family, and meaningful work, but my heart still wanted an anchor, someone to walk beside me. After years of intense focus on survival and rebuilding, I was ready to open myself to love, to the idea of a future built not just on grit and grace, but on a shared foundation with another soul.

This new emotional chapter began with the deceptive brilliance of a cloudless sky. I had returned to college, balancing the demands of my new teaching job with the completion of my degree. Life was full but peaceful, and then he appeared.

The relationship was everything the previous decade had not been; it was simple, straightforward, and filled with promise. He was a steadfast presence, a kind and attentive man who seemed to genuinely cherish my companionship. Our weekends became the highlight of my life. Coming home from college was no longer just a break from studies; it was a return to him. Those long drives along the Louisiana roads, the comfortable silence, and the secure feeling of knowing he would always bring me back safely. These moments felt like a physical embodiment of the care and protection I had yearned for. This was not the tumultuous fire or the blinding grief I had known; this was a gentle, steady rain of contentment.

For more than two years, our relationship felt effortless. There were no storms, no shadows, just steady light. The peace and stability he brought into my life felt almost healing.

After years of loss and uncertainty, being with him made me feel safe again. For the first time in a long while, I was not defined by what I had lost (a son, a job) or what I had endured (shame, surgery), but by the easy happiness of the present.

We talked for hours about everything, our dreams, our plans, our faith. We laughed easily and often. The idea of marriage didn't feel rushed or forced; it felt natural, like the next step in a path that had been quietly unfolding all along. My faith taught me to wait for signs from God, and every part of this relationship felt like one. I truly believed this was His answer to years of prayer.

When we began planning the wedding, my heart overflowed with excitement. Choosing the dress, picturing the ceremony, imagining our life together, it all felt like a beautiful reward after so many hard seasons. I saw our union as a symbol of restoration, proof that grace could rebuild even after deep loss.

When we finally said our vows, surrounded by family and friends, I felt sure that the storms were behind me. Our early years of marriage seemed to confirm it. We were happy, building a quiet, steady life together. It felt like the firm foundation I had long prayed for after the heartbreak of losing David, a place where I could finally rest and believe the sky would stay clear.

A Quiet Shift in the Midst of Blessing

The deepest joy and the true test of any relationship came five years into our marriage with the birth of our first and only daughter. Her arrival changed everything. Holding her for the first time felt like holding a piece of heaven. After all the loss and pain I had endured, she was proof that God could still bring beauty out of ashes. She filled our home with laughter and light, and I often found myself watching her sleep, amazed that such peace could exist after so many storms.

But during that same season of blessing, a quiet shift began to take shape. It wasn't dramatic or obvious at first. It was more like a change in the air, something only the heart could sense. My husband began to change. He became less loving than before, his affection replaced by a curious, unsettling distance. He was still there, still present in the daily routines, but the closeness we once shared began to disappear.

The most painful manifestation of this shift was his attitude toward my physical change. He would stare at me with a coldness that was foreign to the man I married, and he began making statements about my growing stomach. These were not jokes; they were criticisms, small barbs of judgment about the very physical process that had delivered his child.

These words were devastating. They didn't just hurt my feelings; they triggered a deep, familiar wound. I had spent my early life enduring social exclusion and shame due to an unexpected pregnancy. Now, the man who was supposed to be my protector was echoing that same judgment, criticizing the body that had sacrificed to bring life into our world. In those moments, a chilling thought surfaced, a reflection on my son, David, and the sheer amount of grief I had already endured. I knew I had to keep moving. I couldn't afford to be paralyzed by this emotional coldness.

Still, I didn't stop loving him. Instead, I tried harder. I threw myself into being the best wife and mother I could be. I cooked, cleaned, cared for our daughter, and made sure our home ran smoothly. I believed love was something you nurtured through work and sacrifice, the way a farmer tends a field through dry seasons.

Every now and then, the sun would shine again, he would smile, or say something kind, and for a brief moment, I would believe we were finding our way back. Those moments became my fuel, keeping me going through the uncertainty. I convinced myself that it was just a phase, that patience and prayer would bring back the man I once knew.

So, I waited. I prayed. I kept moving forward, trusting that this small cloud would pass. What I didn't realize then was that it was only the beginning of a much greater storm still forming beyond the horizon.

The Slow Erosion of Love

The years that followed were not defined by sudden tragedy but by a slow, constant erosion, a form of water damage to the foundation of the house we had built. There were no explosions or obvious fights, just a gradual fading of warmth and connection.

For nearly two decades, I lived in that in-between space, moving through life with a mix of effort and fragile hope. My days had a steady rhythm: teaching during the day, caring for my daughter in the evenings, and keeping the home running as best I could. I took pride in holding everything together. As long as the house stood, as long as the routines were kept, I convinced myself things were fine.

My sense of worth became tied to keeping life steady. It was the same mindset I had learned working in the factory: be dependable, be diligent, and you will be secure. I believed that if I just worked hard enough at being a good wife and mother, love would stay.

However, inside, the pressure mounted. The cloud of unknowing never entirely lifted. I was perpetually walking on eggshells, trying to anticipate the shift in his mood, interpreting the silence, and searching his eyes for the warmth that used to be so freely given. This constant emotional monitoring was exhausting, a silent, internal storm that chipped away at my spirit every single day. I had survived a fire, I had survived grief, and I had survived a career-ending injury, but I found myself trapped in a state of sustained emotional warfare, fighting for a love that felt increasingly conditional.

During that time, I often turned to the same verse that had carried me before: *"For when I am weak, then am I strong."* But this weakness was not about my body or my circumstances; it was about my heart. I was not facing a disaster from the outside; I was facing the slow breaking of something sacred from within. The strength I needed was not to survive tragedy, but to see the truth behind the life I was pretending was still whole.

The Shattering of Illusion

The illusion of stability finally shattered after twenty-one years. Two decades of effort, sacrifice, and quiet endurance were erased by a single, brutal revelation: He was cheating with multiple partners.

This was the true storm of destruction. It didn't just injure me; it obliterated the entire foundation of my adult life, the shelter I had rebuilt after David's death. The betrayal was not a mistake; it was a sustained pattern of deception that invalidated everything I believed the marriage represented. The very security I had sought, the antidote to my earlier storms, was revealed to be a lie.

The devastation was absolute, but the storm grew worse. The infidelity became aggressively public. One of the women he was involved with began harassing me, my daughter, and even my brother. This was not just a private heartbreak; it was a hostile, external assault on my family. The woman's actions, her open mockery, her intrusion into our lives, represented the ultimate disrespect and amplified the shame I had worked so hard to overcome. I had already endured so much loss in my life, but this was different. It was not a tragedy sent by circumstance; it was a wound inflicted by choice. Seeing my daughter caught in the middle ignited something in me. I realized I couldn't let the chaos continue. My love for my child and the strength I had earned through every past storm gave me the courage to act.

The situation had become unbearable. The trust was gone, the peace was gone, and the emotional weight was too heavy to carry any longer. With tears, prayer, and a painful sense of finality, I made the decision to end the marriage. Filing for divorce was one of the hardest things I had ever done, but in that moment, it was also the only way to protect what little remained of my spirit and my family.

Physical Manifestation of Spiritual Wreckage

The body keeps a record of all the pain the soul endures. After the fire, the factory work, and the years of strain, my body had already been through so much. But nothing compared to the toll this emotional betrayal took. The constant stress, the grief, and the weight of the betrayal finally caused my body to collapse.

I became severely swollen to the point where I could barely move. It was heartbreaking. Here I was, the woman who had survived fire and physical injury, now unable to walk because of emotional pain. The wounds were not caused by anything external; they came from years of mistreatment, neglect, and the absence of love.

This physical breakdown was a sign, one I could no longer ignore. It stripped away the last bit of my self-reliance. I couldn't walk to court. I couldn't stand tall to face the man I had once called my partner. I had to show up in a wheelchair for the final divorce proceedings.

That wheelchair was a powerful symbol of my absolute vulnerability. It was the physical proof that I was, once again, completely and utterly weak. The world, the court system, and the man I married all saw me as broken, a liability, and incapable.

But in that moment, when everything felt like it was falling apart, I heard the comforting truth of Scripture echo in my heart: "*My strength is made perfect in weakness.*"

I understood then that this breakdown was not just destruction, it was a necessary surrender. My first marriage had been the last thing I tried to build on my own strength, on my hard work, sacrifice, and determination. Now, unable to stand on my own, I had no choice but to be carried. My physical weakness was the final step before the renewal of my faith.

I was not drowning in the floodwaters of despair. I was floating, carried by the grace of God. The end of my marriage, the failure of all my human efforts, was the perfect opportunity for God to step in and show His strength. The storm in my heart had broken the sky, but it was not meant to destroy me. It was meant to teach me to rely fully on Him, so that I could build something stronger in His foundation.

A Journey of Recovery

The moment I surrendered in the courtroom, marked by the wheelchair, was just the beginning of a long process of healing, physically and emotionally. My body, worn out by years of internal battles and the recent betrayal, demanded rest. This stillness, at first painful, turned into a time of spiritual reawakening.

Lying in bed, or confined to that chair, I couldn't escape the constant noise in my mind. I had to face the reality of the past twenty-one years. The biggest lie I had believed was that hard work could guarantee happiness. At the factory, my effort earned me a paycheck. In teaching, it earned me a calling. But in my marriage, all my effort, sacrifices, endless work, only kept me trapped in a lie. I had confused endurance with security, thinking that love could be forced through hard work, like a farmer trying to control unpredictable weather.

The healing was not merely about reducing the physical swelling; it was about detoxing my spirit from the poison of betrayal and the shame of failure. The pain in my legs and feet became a constant reminder, a call to lean on God's strength, the only strength that had never let me down.

The day I stood up without pain was not a celebration; it was a quiet victory. The physical therapy wasn't done in a clinic, but at home, with the support of my family's faith. The goal was to regain my independence. The wheelchair had been essential, but it was not where I was meant to stay.

Putting that wheelchair away felt like a spiritual act. It was my final break from the identity of being "broken." By physically standing up, I was declaring that the weakness was gone. The strength I had prayed for was finally here. I was not the woman who had been broken by life's circumstances; I was the woman who had learned to be carried and, in doing so, had found her strength.

My recovery came in small, meaningful steps:

- Walking to the mailbox without help.
- Standing at the stove to cook for my daughter.
- Returning to the classroom, standing in front of my students, teaching not just lessons, but resilience.

Each step was a prayer, a quiet declaration that the ground beneath me, once shattered, was becoming solid again, not from my own efforts, but through God's promise

The New Identity: Woman, Mother, Teacher OR Finding My True Identity

The divorce forced me into a deep reassessment of my identity. I was no longer "Mrs. Richardson," tied to a broken marriage. I was just me, defined by my roles as a mother, a teacher, and a child of God.

The true gift of the divorce was not just freedom from a painful relationship; it was the discovery of unconditional love, the kind I had desperately sought from my husband, but which was freely given by my daughter and my Creator.

My daughter became my focus, the brilliant light in the darkest room. Her presence was the constant, living reminder that my life was fundamentally a success, regardless of the failure of my marriage. The pain from the betrayal became the foundation for a fierce, protective commitment to raising her in an environment of absolute truth and security. I was determined that she would never internalize the message that her worth was conditional or tied to another person's approval.

The experience of my marriage, the slow fading, the sudden betrayal, transformed my work as an educator. I had always been passionate about teaching, but now I carried a deep empathy with me. When a student struggled, I didn't just see frustration with their studies; I saw their deeper struggle.

- I saw the student struggling with a difficult formula, and I recalled the shame of my husband's cold gaze. I taught them: "You are not the test score. You are the effort you put in. Don't let a temporary failure define you."
- I saw the child struggling with a broken family, and I recalled my own loneliness. I taught them: "Your home structure may shift, but your foundation in Christ is unshakable."

My life, with all its failures and lessons, became a vessel for healing. The wreckage of my marriage was not just pain; it became the foundation of everything I taught. I was no longer simply sharing knowledge; I was offering my truth, my strength, and my journey.

The identity I finally embraced was not a self-made one, it was a grace-filled one. I was a woman strong enough to admit that I needed to be carried, and humble enough to pass that strength along to others.

Closure and the Road Ahead

As my body healed and my spirit settled into this new, purposeful identity, I reached a point where I could finally find closure. This was not about ignoring the pain or pretending the past didn't hurt; it was about acknowledging the experience as a necessary storm, one that cleared the way for a new divine plan.

I saw the entire chapter, painful as it was, as an important part of my journey. Even though the marriage ended in heartache, it gave me my daughter. And, in its final years, it forced me to let go of my dependence on human institutions, things like marriage or a steady career, as the ultimate sources of stability.

The financial pressure, though still present, had lessened into a manageable routine. My teaching salary was now enough, and God's quiet provision had made life more manageable. The clouds were beginning to clear completely. The experience of the divorce, the betrayal, and the physical breakdown served as a powerful, final preparation for the next chapter. I realized that though the world had shifted many times, the anchor of my faith had remained steady.

I was not just surviving anymore. I was thriving, learning to live fully in my weakness. Being single and independent no longer felt like a daunting void. Instead, it became a road full of possibilities. With a foundation of grace, I felt ready for whatever challenges or storms lay ahead. The quiet strength I had gained was the result of the painful journey through the First Storm of the Heart.

The true measure of my healing was my decision to look forward, not backward. I was no longer bound by the past. The next step in my life, the next chapter, was waiting to be written.

Chapter 6

The Storm of the Unknown Killer

Life had finally grown still again. My daughter was thriving, my classroom was steady, and I was beginning to believe that peace had taken root for good. After so many storms, the quiet felt sacred, almost fragile. I thought I had learned all that pain could teach me. But peace, I would soon learn, is not the end of the story; it is often the calm before another tempest.

The quiet strength I had pieced together after all storms was delicate. I had taught myself to stand again, believing the worst was behind me: the emotional tempests, the searing grief, the fires that nearly consumed me. But I was wrong. The next storm didn't creep in like a heavy sky; it hit like a violent squall, sudden and merciless, and it shattered my sense of safety. Losing my oldest brother, Jr., was a different kind of devastation. It was not just grief; it was a storm laced with malice and unresolved pain, and it shook the foundation I had only just begun to rebuild.

I had no reason to expect another heartbreak, no warning that the ground beneath me was about to give way again. The days felt ordinary, peaceful even, which is often how tragedy hides, just beyond the horizon of normal life.

Signs in the Silence

It began, as tragedies often do, with a perfectly ordinary day that ended with a conversation that now haunts my memory. My brother, Jr., was going through the painful separation from his wife at the time, and his heart was breaking because he desperately missed his children. That night, he called me because he needed to hear a familiar, steady voice, someone who wouldn't judge but would simply listen. I could feel the weight of his sadness, a tangible burden of anxiety and loneliness, even through the telephone line.

"I'm coming home to see y'all," he told me, his voice rough with despair and urgency, and I tried to be the anchor, as I always tried to be. "It'll be okay with time, Buddy," I told him, trying to soothe the raw edges of his pain. I spoke about the future, about how things always look better when you can hold your children again, trying to pull him forward out of the darkness he was sinking into.

Then he stopped talking for a long, heavy minute. The silence on the other end stretched, heavy and unnatural. I had heard him sad before, but this was different; it felt final. "Buddy, are you still there?" I asked, a knot tightening in my stomach.

"Yes," he finally replied, his voice strained and quiet, devoid of its usual playful resilience. Then the words came out with a desperate, chilling insistence: "Listen to me, I want my children back." He was not arguing for a custody battle; he was pleading for connection, for a return to normalcy that felt unreachable. Then, completely out of the blue, he said something that was a chilling premonition, a farewell I was too stunned to recognize in the moment: "If anything happens to me, I want my children to have everything I own."

I was used to his unexpected declarations, but this felt different, and it gave me a profound pause. It sounded like a man signing off. I tried desperately to pull us back to solid ground, to laugh it off. "Buddy," I replied, trying to sound casual, even slightly annoyed, "I'm sure they'll get all of your inheritance when the time comes. Don't worry like that. You're coming home." We hung up shortly after, with the simple, heartbreaking promise of seeing him soon. I did not know that was the last time I would ever hear his voice. That call was the calm before the tempest.

I hung up that night feeling uneasy, but I brushed it off, trusting that prayer and time would heal him. I didn't realize that I had just said goodbye.

Less than a day later, the calm that followed our call would be torn apart by the first gusts of a storm I could never have imagined.

The Moment Everything Shattered

The phone call that shattered the peace came not even twenty-four hours later: he had been shot. The news was fragmented, chaotic, and terrifying, the kind of confusing information that denies immediate belief. We didn't know where he was. In the initial panic, one person told us he was in a hospital in Mansfield, Louisiana, but that was false. We rushed there only to find nothing. Next, we were told he was at his mother-in-law's house, which was where his wife and children were staying.

My first cousin drove my car to the address, and the scene that greeted us was overwhelming, a shock to the system. We arrived in the dark, and the night was sliced apart by the flashing blue and red lights of multiple police cars, illuminating the yard and the porch in sickening, intermittent flashes. There were so many police officers, so many people standing in small, stunned groups; neighbors, officials, silent witnesses. The atmosphere was charged with a terrible, silent violence, the air thick with fear and the incomprehensible reality of crime. We learned they had moved him from the front porch, and the police now told us they had taken him to Shreveport, Louisiana.

We were frantic, still clinging to the thread of hope that he was just wounded, trying to find out what hospital he was taken to, desperately searching for a place, any place, where we could simply sit down and wait for a sign that he was fighting for his life. Then the investigating officer came over to where our small group was huddled. He was a large man, impersonal and efficient, and he looked directly at me. He delivered the blunt, unforgiving truth that stopped my heart: "He's dead."

Oh, that moment. That was when I felt the full force of the storm hit, not like a gust of wind, but like the shattering of my entire reality. I saw the lightning flashing, I felt the high wind blowing, and I felt the floodwaters of despair wash over me. The location where it all took place—Holly, Louisiana, on the obscure Bradshaw Road—became instantly sacred and tragic, the place where my brother's life ended far too soon, a single, lonely spot forever marked by violence.

The profound, ongoing pain of this tragedy was magnified by the horrifying fact that the killer was unknown; a shadow, a ghost. The police had secured the scene, but they offered no immediate answers, no clear suspects, only questions and paperwork. We were left in a limbo of grief and utter helplessness.

In the days that followed, the storm was not just the shock of what had happened; it was the relentless, suffocating pressure of not knowing what came next. We waited for answers that never arrived. The person who took my brother's life remained a shadow, a haunting presence that hovered over our family. It felt cruel and unreal, knowing his life had ended so violently, and yet there was no closure, no justice, just silence.

The investigation felt distant and cold. We, the grieving family, felt like outside observers to our own tragedy. We were desperate for a name, a motive, anything to make sense of the senseless, but the details were locked away in police files, only deepening our frustration and fear. The very title of this storm, *The Unknown Killer*, became synonymous with a cruel kind of torment, reminding us daily that the person responsible for destroying our family was still walking free.

The hours that followed blurred together: sirens, questions, and silence. But even in the chaos, one thought pressed through every other: I had to tell Mother.

The hardest part of any storm isn't the first strike of lightning; it's the moment you realize you must deliver that same bolt to someone you love.

The Hardest Words I Ever Spoke

I remember standing there, knowing that the hardest task was still ahead: I had to tell Mother. This was not just delivering a message; it was delivering a blow, a strike designed to knock the foundation out from under her. The internal dread I felt on the drive to her house was worse than any physical pain I had ever endured.

When I finally told her, my storm of pain arrived with high winds that would take the very breath out of your body. She initially refused to believe it, her mind simply rejecting the impossibility of the news. Then, the reality crashed over her. The way she cried was not just weeping; it was a sound of total breakdown, a primal scream of loss. It truly looked like the floodgates of her soul had just opened, releasing decades of hidden grief and fear. And there was nothing I could do to stem the tide.

In the midst of her inconsolable grief, she passed out. In an instant, the focus shifted from the external tragedy to an immediate, terrifying, and internal crisis. That was yet another storm: trying to take care of her in the paralyzing, life-threatening loss of her child.

Then there was my other brother, Junior's namesake, consumed by a fierce, blinding rage fueled by grief and the injustice of it all. He was crying so hard, consumed by the desire for revenge. I was crying, too, trying to hold myself together while tending to Mother and restraining him simultaneously. In that impossible, fractured moment, I could feel the powerful, steady hand of God carrying me. It was a brief, unmistakable moment of supernatural strength gifted just when I needed it most to prevent utter collapse. People began coming from everywhere, thank God, a community of comfort in the chaos. The males in the family took over working with my brother, trying desperately to convince him to calm down and not to make things worse for our fragile mother.

We had to take Mother to the emergency room, not for a physical injury, but to manage her emotions. She was in a state of shock, repeating only two words, over and over: "My child. My child." She kept repeating the heartbreaking irony that tore at her soul: "He went to war in Vietnam and bullets were all around him, and he came home and got killed by a bullet." It was the ultimate betrayal of safety. She was so weak, calling him "Jr." over and over, as if the repetition would bring him back. The wind was blowing, the lightning flashing, and the floodwaters of sorrow were truly rolling. It was a big storm filled with incomprehensible pain that threatened to claim her life, too.

Grief doesn't pause to let you breathe; it simply shifts shape. One moment you're holding your mother's shaking hands, and the next, you're signing papers and making choices no one is ever ready for.

The Storm of Arrangements

Next came the storm of logistics and expense: making the funeral arrangements. Junior's wife, my sister-in-law, was understandably paralyzed by grief and shock. The burden of decision-making fell to us, the shattered pieces of his immediate family.

It was a moment of true grace from an unexpected place that shone through the rain. The funeral director, a woman of deep compassion who was a relative of my sister-in-law, had recently lost her own brother. She looked at my mother and me with profound, personal empathy. "We're all in it together," she told her gently, her voice cutting through the panic. "Let's make the arrangements now, before the grief consumes us." That simple phrase, acknowledging our shared, terrible experience, was a moment of deep, human kindness that helped to part the clouds momentarily.

His three children, my beloved nieces and nephew, were with us, forced into a cruel and adult reality. In a heartbreaking display of resilience, we involved them in every decision, letting them make the painful selections for their father's service, choosing the casket, the programs, the final details. The storm kept on rising; it was time to plan for the costs and everything that comes with burying a loved one suddenly. We knew absolutely nothing about his business affairs or his estate; all we knew was the place where he worked. The embarrassment of admitting this felt like another wave of shame washing over us.

Again, the funeral director's grace was a quiet, profound miracle in the devastation. I will never forget her words. Recognizing our absolute helplessness and our financial uncertainty, she simply said, "Don't worry," her voice firm and assuring. "I'm going to bury him." Her quiet assurance was a lifeline, a divine provision when all human systems had failed. It was an act of God's grace, channeled through her humanity, that allowed us to focus on our grief instead of our deficits.

By the time we reached the day of his service, exhaustion had taken hold, but so had a strange calm. The worst had already happened; all that was left was to honor him and somehow keep breathing through it.

A Moment of Surrender

At his service, there were so many people, a powerful testament to the life he had lived and the community he had built. His pastor and the male chorus came all the way from Houston, Texas. They sang, and the atmosphere in the room was thick with sorrow and faith, a shared burden of grief that somehow made the weight bearable.

The music was meant to comfort, but the final song, his favorite, broke me. The male chorus sang **"Mother Bowed."** When they reached the final, powerful verse, something inside me just broke. The sky busted wide open, and the floodwaters of my stored-up emotion were flowing in a way I had never seen before. I had been strong for Mother, for my younger brother, for the children. I had held the line. But in that moment, I lost it.

I was physically sobbing, doubled over, completely undone. I didn't know where they had taken my mother, nor did I know where the children and my brother were. Everything felt utterly chaotic and out of control. My vision blurred with tears, and the voices around me turned into a desperate, unintelligible hum. This was a tragedy that I didn't know how I was going to get through. I was no longer the one holding others up; I was the one drowning.

But when it was all over, when the final words were spoken and he was finally laid to rest, I could feel God carrying me. In the moment I had completely lost hope, in the wake of the deepest storm of my heart, His power was made perfect in my weakness. The storm of the unknown killer had tried to drown me, but instead, it taught me that even in the absolute wreckage of life, even when the human foundation is ripped out, there is an invisible, steady hand that never fails to lift you up and carry you through.

When the final song faded and silence filled the sanctuary, the storm felt as if it had finally spent itself. But grief doesn't vanish when the music stops; it lingers quietly, reshaping the days that follow.

My brother had died in August 1984, leaving behind three children who needed their aunt more than ever, and a foundation of pain that would quickly lead to the next great storm. The tragedy of Junior's death was compounded by the nature of his murder: a death by an unknown assailant. The storm did not end with the burial; it settled into a low, cold drizzle of unresolved pain. The police investigation was a source of constant frustration. Leads went nowhere. The initial chaos never resolved into clarity.

Unresolved Shadows

Weeks turned into months, and still the questions remained. The mystery itself became its own grinding, ongoing storm. The lack of justice was like sand in the wound, preventing any clean scar from forming. Every time a question went unanswered, every time a new theory surfaced, it was a fresh jolt of lightning. We were not allowed the closure of a known truth. We lived, and still live, with the crushing weight of the unknown killer, a malevolent shadow perpetually cast over our memories of Jr. It was the hardest thing to preach to my family: to surrender the need for human justice and trust in a justice that existed beyond the courtroom. The very core of our family peace was eroded by this agonizing wait for an answer that never came.

My brother's death left an ache that time could not seal, a wound made deeper by the unanswered questions that followed. Yet even as the mystery endured, I began to see that faith itself is not built on explanations but on endurance. The same hand that carried me through fire and betrayal carried me once more through this storm. I did not know it then, but this loss would prepare me for the next great reckoning of my life, a storm that would test not only my faith, but the limits of my endurance and the depth of my surrender.

Chapter 7

The Aftermath: The Death of My Mother

Nine years had passed since my brother Junior was taken from us, and life had settled into a fragile, delicate rhythm. The world outside seemed ordinary, even calm, but inside our hearts, the unanswered questions of his death lingered like a shadow that refused to lift. The unknown killer's face, unseen and unpunished, haunted us in quiet moments and loud ones alike. Each year brought its own reminder that the pain of loss was not something that ever truly left; it simply changed shape, hiding in corners, lying dormant until something stirred it awake. Our family had learned to live with this shadow, to breathe around it, to function even while carrying it. But time, as it does, never fully heals; it only teaches us to carry our grief with us in ways that seem survivable.

During those years, my mother had moved from her home in the country to a senior citizen apartment just three blocks from my own house. It had been her choice, one made with a mixture of desire and necessity. She wanted independence, yet she wanted to be close enough that if something went wrong, someone would be nearby. I had been cautiously optimistic about this move, imagining that perhaps the distance from old routines and memories might ease her heart, that the closeness to me and my daughter might provide a quiet reassurance. It was supposed to be a peaceful chapter, a gentle season in which we could enjoy life as best we could together yet apart, near yet maintaining our own worlds.

Every day, my daughter and I would make our way to her apartment, small rituals that became the backbone of our routines. Some mornings, we brought coffee; other times, I would cook a plate of food and carry it over, my husband often joining us to share in the small comforts of family life. These visits were simple, almost mundane, yet beneath the surface, they were threads holding us together. Each smile, each small conversation, each meal carried unspoken affirmations: *We are still here. We are still family. We still love each other.* For a while, these gestures seemed enough. Mother seemed lighter, happier. Her laughter returned in quiet moments, her eyes sparkled with fleeting warmth, and I allowed myself to believe that perhaps the worst storms of our lives were behind us.

But grief, I would come to remember, is not bound by timelines or expectations. It does not recognize calm, and it does not respect peace. Just when the mind begins to let its guard down, when the heart begins to imagine safety, the storm can arrive without warning.

I still remember the day it came, how ordinary it began, and how utterly catastrophic it became. I had returned home from work, preparing for the usual evening routine with my daughter, packing lunches, helping with homework, and tucking her in for the night. The house was quiet, almost serene. And then the phone rang. It was Mother. Her voice, usually steady and warm, was sharp with urgency, trembling with fear and exhaustion. "I'm as sick as I can be," she said, each word hanging in the line like a warning bell. The thunder rumbled in the distance, and the wind whipped against the windows as though the world itself had heard her cry and was responding.

Something in my chest tightened, an instinctive, gut-level knowing that this was no ordinary illness, no temporary weakness. I grabbed my daughter's hand, my heart already racing, and we ran to her apartment. The moment I opened the door, my worst fears were confirmed. There she was, lying on the floor, fragile, trembling, her body helpless beneath the weight of a storm I could not yet see in its entirety. It was a scene that would forever be etched into my memory: the fear, the panic, the uncontrollable flood of emotion that swept through me as though it were a hurricane tearing through everything I had built to protect her.

The Storm of the Emergency

When I arrived, the sight that met me shattered every sense of normalcy. Mother lay on the floor, her body limp, her face pale and drawn. I dropped to my knees beside her, lifting her trembling frame, whispering prayers between the tears that streamed down my cheeks. "Mother, stay with me. God is here," I begged, as my daughter held onto my leg, her small hands gripping me tightly, wide-eyed, frozen in a mix of fear and awe at the storm that had suddenly overtaken our lives.

The paramedics arrived swiftly, their movements precise and efficient, cutting through my panic with calm authority. They lifted Mother onto the stretcher, and I followed, holding her hand, murmuring prayers over her as the ambulance doors shut behind us. The ride to the hospital was a blur of sirens, shaking, and whispered promises to God that she would not be taken from us. My daughter sat quietly in the backseat, clutching her doll, her eyes large and shining with the same fear I felt coursing through my own veins.

Warnings in the Beating Heart

At the hospital, the storm intensified, each moment heavy with an unbearable weight. Nurses and doctors moved around Mother with swift precision, their motions practiced and efficient, yet to me, they were a flurry of chaos I could not control. Monitors beeped, blood pressure cuffs tightened, and the air itself seemed charged, electric, trembling with the urgency of a life hanging by a thread. The waiting room was no longer just a space of waiting; it became a place where time stretched and warped, minutes dragging into hours, each second a reminder of the fragility of the ones we love most.

I called my brother, my voice shaking, my words rushing out in fragments as I tried to explain the situation. "You need to come," I said.

"She's not well... it's serious." He arrived quickly, the familiar tension in his shoulders matching my own. Together, we hovered near her bed, holding her hands, stroking her hair, whispering prayers and words of encouragement, trying in some way to anchor her and ourselves in the midst of a storm that had suddenly overturned our lives. My daughter stayed close by, her small fingers gripping mine, her wide eyes reflecting the fear she could not yet name. Even at her age, she understood that something terrible had happened, something that had shifted the very ground beneath us.

The doctor arrived, his face grave, his expression a combination of professional detachment and human concern. He reviewed the results of the tests and x-rays with measured, calm language, but to us, each word felt like a blow. "Your mother is at risk of a stroke," he said, his voice steady but heavy with implication. My heart sank into a pit of dread. A stroke? Already, the storm had shifted from urgent concern to something far more terrifying, something that carried the power to destroy in an instant. I could feel my knees weakening, the room tilting as though the floors themselves were giving way beneath me.

He paused, letting the weight of the words settle before continuing. "She will need to be admitted to the ICU immediately," he said. The words hung in the air, sharp and cutting, and I could see the panic mirrored in my brother's eyes. Our mother, who had always been strong, always the center of calm in our storms, now needed us to be strong for her in ways I had never imagined. Before we could even digest that news, the doctor returned with another blow, one that spun the room further into chaos: "She will need to be airlifted to the trauma hospital in Shreveport. It is the only way we can ensure her survival."

I felt the words hit me like a tornado, spinning my thoughts into a blur of panic, disbelief, and fear. Airlifted. Trauma hospital. My mind raced, trying to make sense of what it meant, trying to find some foothold in the storm, some way to protect the woman who had always been the anchor of our family. I glanced at my brother, whose hands were gripping the railing of the hospital bed so tightly that his knuckles were white. His face was pale, eyes wide, reflecting the same helplessness I felt. My daughter clung to me, quiet now, her small body trembling, sensing that this storm was far larger than any she had ever seen.

The nurses moved quickly, preparing her for transport, checking her IVs, adjusting monitors, and ensuring every life-saving measure was in place. I whispered over her, my voice breaking, "Hold on, Mother. Please, just hold on. God is with you." Her eyes fluttered open briefly, a faint smile touching her lips, a fragile thread of reassurance that she understood we were there, that we were praying, that we would not let her go alone.

But the storm would not wait. The helicopter was scheduled, a massive machine of metal and noise, ready to carry her away to Shreveport. As we made preparations, my brother and I exchanged frantic glances, hearts pounding with fear and uncertainty. The sound of rotors approaching filled the air, a terrifying roar that mirrored the panic in our chests. My hands shook so badly I could barely hold her, my daughter's small fingers wrapped tightly around mine, both of us grounded only by the prayers we whispered through tears.

And then, the heart monitor sounded a flatline. The beeping stopped, replaced by a silence so complete it was deafening. She was gone. The tornado of our lives touched down fully, devastating everything in its path. My brother fell to his knees, my daughter screamed, and I collapsed beside her, my cries blending with the storm outside, with the wind, the rain, the thunder, all of it an echo of the hurricane that had claimed the one person who had always been our steady center.

Even as paramedics worked frantically, checking for any sign, any spark of life, I knew the truth. The storm had won. My heart felt as though it had been ripped from my chest, shredded by the winds of grief. And yet, amidst the destruction, I whispered a prayer, holding my daughter close: *God, give us the strength to survive this hurricane. Carry us through what we cannot endure alone.*

Facing the Decisions Alone

And once again, on November 14, 1993, I found myself standing at the doors of the funeral home, a place already etched into my memory from the losses of my brother and my son. The familiarity brought no comfort this time, only the weight of inevitability. I had arrived not just to plan a service, but to face the reality that the woman who had always been my anchor, my guide, my protector, was gone. Mother could not walk these halls with me, could not lift her voice to help make decisions, could not be the steady hand I had leaned on so many times before. I was alone in carrying the responsibility, and the storm inside me threatened to break through every layer of composure I had left.

The funeral director greeted me with quiet compassion, her presence a small light in the overwhelming darkness. She knew grief, had seen it in its many forms, and I felt the first glimmer of relief that someone else could carry some of this unbearable weight. Together, we walked through caskets, examining each one with a care that made the finality almost tangible. I ran my hands over the polished wood, imagining Mother resting there, imagining the moment when I would have to say goodbye one last time. Each choice, a casket, a floral arrangement, a program, felt monumental, as though my very hands were shaping the memory of her life.

I thought of my daughter, of my brother, of the family who would gather to honor her. I thought of the hours we had spent together, the quiet lessons she had taught me about faith, resilience, and love. Now, it was my turn to honor her life in a way she could no longer participate in, and the weight was crushing. Every decision felt like a tidal wave, threatening to sweep me under. I whispered prayers under my breath, asking God for guidance, asking for strength to stand when I wanted to collapse.

At one point, I paused, leaning against the edge of a display, closing my eyes to hold back the tears that threatened to spill over. My chest ached, my heart felt raw and open, and yet, somehow, I felt Him there carrying me, sustaining me in the moment my flesh could not. God's presence was quiet but undeniable, a steady hand holding mine as I made decisions I would have otherwise been too weak to face.

By the time the arrangements were made, exhaustion had taken its toll, but so had a strange sense of calm. The hurricane of grief still raged, but for a moment, I felt the grounding of God's grace. Each selection I had made was an act of love, a final tribute to a life well-lived, a life that had shaped the family and me in ways too profound to measure. Even in the devastation, there was purpose, there was a way to honor her memory with dignity, and there was God, lifting me when I could not lift myself.

Church Services

Mother's homegoing celebration was nothing short of extraordinary. The day was bright, almost defiant against the storm of sorrow that had followed us for so long. More than fifty years of faithful service as an usher, Sunday school teacher, and mission member had touched countless lives, and on this day, those lives gathered to honor her. The church was filled with faces, both familiar and beloved friends, family, church members, and even strangers whose lives had been shaped by her quiet acts of devotion.

The air was thick with emotion. Each hug, each whispered word of sympathy, each tear shed was a reminder of the depth of her impact. People spoke with reverence and warmth, painting a portrait of a woman whose life had been a testament to love, faith, and unwavering commitment. Stories of her generosity, her laughter, and her steady guidance were shared, each one echoing like a gentle bell through the sanctuary. I watched, holding my daughter close, feeling the enormity of what we had lost, yet also sensing the remarkable legacy Mother left behind.

The music rose, carrying with it the melodies she had loved, each note weaving memories into the air. The male chorus, the organ, the voices of the congregation all combined to lift the weight of grief into something bearable, something transcendent. I found myself smiling through tears as I saw the joy and reverence in the faces around me. For a moment, it didn't feel like a funeral. It felt like a celebration, a life fully lived and fully loved, a soul returning home.

As the service progressed, I felt a strange sense of relief, a quiet lifting in the midst of the storm. God's presence was tangible, a steady, invisible hand holding me upright when I felt my knees give way. I could feel Him carrying not only me but the entire congregation, sustaining us as we honored her memory. It was as though each song, each eulogy, each prayer, was a thread weaving a safety net under our collective grief.

When it came time to lay her to rest, the cemetery at New Hope Baptist Church became a place of sacred reunion. Mother was laid to rest alongside my son, my father, my grandmother, and my brother, a family united even in eternity. Standing there, surrounded by the familiar gravestones and the echoing words of prayer, I felt the continuity of love, the unbroken line of faith, and the power of God's grace that had carried us through every storm.

Mother passed away at the age of seventy-eight. Her life had been long, faithful, and full. She had been our anchor, the quiet force holding our family together. Even in her passing, she left a testament to strength, devotion, and faith. Her life, her service, and her unwavering love reminded me that God's hand never abandons us, even in the midst of the fiercest storms.

PART FOUR

RISING THROUGH THE RUINS

Chapter 8

Rising Beyond the Grip of Grief

After Mother's passing, time seemed to stop. The house felt quieter than it ever had before, too quiet, the kind of quiet that presses on your chest and makes you aware of every breath you take. The echo of her voice lingered in the corners of every room, and the faint scent of her perfume would sometimes drift through unexpectedly, pulling me back into memories I wasn't ready to face.

Each morning, I woke up and went through the motions, making breakfast, getting my daughter ready, and showing up for work, but it felt like I was living outside of myself. My heart was somewhere else, caught in a place between presence and memory. I was functioning, but not living. The grief had built a paralysis around me, a kind of invisible wall that kept me from seeing anything beyond the loss.

For months, I existed in that stillness, trapped between what was and what could be. There was no storm, no wind, just the eerie calm that comes after destruction, when the world holds its breath, unsure if the worst is truly over. I remember sitting one night at the edge of my bed, my daughter asleep beside me, thinking about all the people I had lost: my brother, my son, my mother, and wondering how much more my heart could endure. I whispered a prayer into the silence, asking God to either take away the pain or show me what to do with it.

That prayer was the beginning of the shift.

It didn't come as a sudden revelation or a miracle moment. It was subtle, like the first glimmer of sunrise touching the horizon after a long night. One morning, I woke up and realized that I didn't want my story to end with grief. I didn't want my daughter to grow up watching me drown in sorrow. I wanted her to see that life could rise again, that faith could breathe life into the ashes of loss.

That thought ignited something inside me, a spark of purpose, small but steady. It whispered that maybe healing wasn't about forgetting, but about moving with the memory, learning to walk again even when your legs still tremble.

So, I began to think about what I could do to move forward. I had always loved teaching, helping children learn, and seeing their faces light up with understanding. It was something that made me feel alive, connected. I already had my degree in *Early Childhood Education*, but my work in the school system extended beyond the younger grades. To continue teaching the students I was serving from first through eighth grade, I needed certification in *Elementary Education*.

The idea of returning to school seemed impossible at first. How could I study when I could barely focus? How could I chase a goal when I still felt shattered? But something inside me urged me on; perhaps it was the same faith that had carried me through every storm before.

I decided to leap.

Enrolling in classes was like stepping out into sunlight after being hidden away in the dark. For the first time in months, I had something to look forward to, something that wasn't defined by loss. The textbooks, the lectures, the assignments, all of it reminded me that my mind was still capable, that I still had a purpose beyond my pain.

It wasn't easy. Some days, the grief returned like a sudden gust of wind, knocking the breath out of me. There were moments when I would look up from my notes and see my mother's face in my mind, smiling proudly as if she were saying, *Keep going, daughter. You're doing just fine.* And then there were nights when exhaustion and loneliness crept in, when I missed her so deeply that I could barely hold the pen steady in my hand.

But each time I felt the weight pressing down, I prayed. And each time, I felt God lifting it, even if just enough to take the next step.

Slowly, the stillness that had once held me captive began to loosen. I found myself laughing again quietly, cautiously, but genuinely. I found joy in my daughter's laughter, in my students' progress, in the way life continued to unfold despite everything I had lost. I was learning that healing wasn't a single act but a daily decision to get up, to try, to believe.

Finding Life in Learning Again

Enrolling in those classes was both terrifying and exhilarating. It was like stepping out into the sunlight after months of rain, blinking against the brightness but grateful to feel warmth again. Each class, each lecture, became a symbol of hope, a quiet reminder that I was still capable of building, of growing, of rising after everything that had fallen apart.

There was a sense of renewal in walking across a campus again, books in hand, surrounded by the hum of life and learning. For the first time in a long while, I felt connected to something forward-moving. My grief didn't disappear; it lingered, like an ache in the background, but now it existed alongside purpose. I found meaning in the small victories: passing an exam, completing an assignment, or simply understanding a new concept that would help me become a better teacher.

The days were long, and the nights often longer, but every moment carried a quiet determination. There were times I had to bring my daughter to class with me because I had no one else to keep her. She would sit beside me with crayons and paper, her small presence a source of both comfort and motivation. I missed my mother deeply in those moments. I could almost hear her voice telling me to keep going, to stay strong, to remember that storms don't last forever.

There were hard days, too, the kind that made me question if I was strong enough to keep pushing forward. Days when exhaustion crept in, when tears blurred the ink on my notebook, and when my heart longed for the familiar comfort of my mother's steady presence. But even in those moments, I could feel God carrying me. His strength filled the spaces where mine ran out, guiding me step by step, like sunlight breaking through the clouds after a long storm.

Sometimes, in the middle of teaching, a student would say something innocent and unknowingly that reminded me of her. It could be a phrase she used to say, a smile that mirrored her warmth, or simply the sound of laughter in the room. When that happened, I would step away for a moment, letting the tears come quietly, allowing the floodwaters of memory to flow. But when I returned, I felt renewed, refreshed, as though God Himself had washed away the heaviness and filled me with peace.

The Work of Purpose

The California Achievement Test, or CAT, was more than just an exam to me; it became a mirror of life's tests. Each year, the results determined which students needed extra academic help, identifying those who scored below fifty percent and placing them in supplemental programs for remediation. Many teachers saw it as a routine part of the school system, another metric to manage. But for me, it became a sacred responsibility. These were not just students who had fallen behind; they were children carrying their own quiet storms, much like the one I was trying to survive.

Every morning, as I stepped into the classroom, I carried both my lesson plans and the lingering ache of loss. The desks, lined neatly in rows, became small altars where I poured out patience, encouragement, and love. Each child had a story, a reason their test score didn't reflect their worth. Some came from broken homes, some struggled with learning disabilities, and others were simply lost in the noise of life. I saw myself in their uncertainty. They were fighting to find their footing, just as I was fighting to find mine.

Teaching those students filled the hollow places in my spirit that grief had carved out. Every time one of them grasped a new concept or read a sentence with newfound confidence, I felt a spark of healing inside me. It was as if God was whispering, "See? There is still purpose here. There is still beauty in what you can give."

I poured myself into my work with a passion that surprised even me. I spent late nights creating materials, searching for new ways to reach each child. Sometimes I would sit with one student long after the final bell had rung, helping them sound out words, explaining fractions, or simply listening to them talk about their day. In those quiet moments, I realized that my classroom had become both a sanctuary and a therapy room for them, and for me.

My students taught me lessons that no textbook could hold. They reminded me that progress often looks like persistence, not perfection. Those small victories, like finishing a page of reading without tears, were worth celebrating. They showed me the strength that comes from getting up every day, no matter how heavy the heart feels. And in return, I gave them everything I had: encouragement, structure, laughter when I could find it, and grace when they stumbled.

There were days when the memories of my mother would rise without warning. A word, a song from the hallway, or even the sound of children's laughter could open the floodgates. When that happened, I would excuse myself for a moment, step into the hallway, and let the tears fall silently. I would pray there, leaning against the cool wall, asking God for strength to keep going. And every single time, He met me there in the quiet, in the exhaustion, in the small act of choosing to return to the classroom and keep teaching.

The storms of grief and purpose often collided, but I learned to let them coexist. Grief didn't vanish simply because I found something meaningful to do. Instead, it transformed. It softened, reshaped itself into compassion, and gave me a deeper understanding of the human heart. When I looked into the eyes of my struggling students, I saw not failure, but potential. I saw the reflection of a God who doesn't measure us by where we fall short, but by how we rise.

Looking back, I can see how those classroom days shaped more than my career; they shaped my recovery. The laughter of children became my therapy. Their small triumphs became my reminders that light could return after darkness. The work of lifting others became the way God lifted me.

Winds of Responsibility

The journey was not easy. Every day felt like walking against a relentless wind, steady, unyielding, determined to test my strength. Without Mother there to help care for my daughter, I had to learn to juggle more than I ever thought possible. There were mornings when I would pack both our bags, one filled with textbooks and lesson plans, the other with crayons, snacks, and storybooks. She would sit quietly in the back of my classroom or beside me in the lecture hall, her small presence both a comfort and a reminder of why I had to keep going.

I was a wife, a mother, a student, and a teacher, and somehow, I had to be all four at once. There were days I felt like I was failing at each of them. I would wake before dawn to prepare lessons, rush to work, attend classes, and return home to cook, clean, and care for my family. Sleep was a luxury I rarely tasted. Yet even in the exhaustion, there was something sacred in the struggle. Each breath, each step forward, was proof that God's strength was greater than my weariness.

When I sat in class, I took notes with one hand while holding my daughter close with the other. She would look up at me with sleepy eyes, and I'd whisper a silent prayer of thanks that she was patient, that God had given me a child who understood the quiet battles her mother was fighting. The professors knew my situation, and some would smile kindly when they saw her beside me, an unspoken acknowledgment that this, too, was education.

Some nights, when the tears came without warning after long days of teaching children who reminded me of my mother's gentleness, or when loneliness crept in like the evening wind. On those nights, I would open my Bible and read until peace settled over me again. I clung to faith like an anchor, trusting that the God who had carried me through storms of loss would not abandon me now in this storm of responsibility.

Chapter 9

The End of a New Beginning

During this time in my life, I was faced with many storms. The last few years of my first marriage were rough and rocky. The storms were heavy, filled with wind, thunderstorms, lightning, and flooding at times. The more I tried to make my marriage work, the more he worked against me. The cheating and violence escalated, and I found myself sinking deeper into depression. I kept searching for hope, for something to hold on to. I turned to God, the only source I knew, as I had done before during other storms. He had carried me through turbulent times in the past, and I trusted Him to carry me through this one, too. But what I wanted, more than anything, was for God to change him, to make him treat me as a wife, to make things better for our daughter.

We still had our daughter to raise, and I kept praying that somehow, someway, things would change. But no matter how much I prayed, no matter how hard I tried to fix things, the storm only grew worse. The emotional, mental, and physical toll on me was unbearable. Instead of change, I watched as he continued to make choices that further destroyed what was left of our marriage. My body, mind, and spirit all began to break down. It felt as though the very foundation of our lives was crumbling, piece by piece, and I was helpless to stop it. The anger, the bitterness, the lies, it was all too much. I didn't know how to fight anymore.

I wanted God to change him, to make him see me, to make him love me, but instead, God moved me out. It wasn't what I wanted, but it was what I needed. The choice wasn't mine to make, but it was the beginning of my healing. I had to leave. I had to step away from the abuse, from the storms that had torn me apart. The decision felt like a betrayal of everything I had once believed in marriage, family, love, but it was the only way to save myself, to save my daughter.

The weeks that followed were filled with an overwhelming mix of emotions. I was devastated, heartbroken, and exhausted. I had lost my identity as a wife, and I felt like I was drifting in a sea of uncertainty. I didn't know who I was anymore. I had been so consumed by the storms of my marriage that I had forgotten how to be me. But as I navigated this new reality, I began to feel the first stirrings of hope, the faintest glimpse of the sun peeking through the clouds. God, in His own way, had carried me through the darkest moment of my life and was leading me toward something new.

The Breaking Point

Before I left, I went through a period where one of the women my husband was chatting with began targeting not only me, but my daughter and my brother as well. It felt like I was being surrounded by this toxic force, and I could no longer keep fighting. That was the straw that broke the camel's back. It wasn't just a straw; it was like a bale of hay that hit me all at once, knocking me over, leaving me with no strength to stand. I couldn't endure it any longer.

The emotional and physical toll this marriage had taken on me was overwhelming. It wasn't just the infidelity or the emotional abuse; it was the constant fear, the constant tension, the knowing that no matter how hard I tried to hold everything together, the ground underneath me was always shifting. The weight of it all bore down on me, like a storm cloud that wouldn't leave.

The stress from the marriage caused my body to break down in ways I had never experienced before. I started swelling all over, my joints and limbs becoming pained and stiff, as if my body was trying to carry the weight of all the pain I had endured. My physical condition deteriorated rapidly. I lost my ability to care for myself, and everything seemed like it was slipping out of my control. My teeth were knocked out during one of the many violent altercations, and I felt humiliated, beaten down, and utterly lost.

It was then that I went to see my doctor, someone I had trusted for years. His reaction when he saw what I had endured was nothing short of devastating. His face registered disbelief, anger, and genuine sorrow. "A man you were married to did this to you?" he asked, his voice filled with a mix of shock and frustration. I couldn't even answer him. There were no words to explain what I had been through, and in that moment, I realized just how far gone everything had become. His words cut through me: "If you don't get a divorce from this man, do not come back to my office for anything."

It was the final push I needed. His ultimatum, though harsh, was a wake-up call. It was the moment I understood that I couldn't keep going in this cycle of pain and abuse. I had spent years praying for God to change him, to make him a better man, a better husband, a better father. But God's answer came not in the form of a changed man, but in the form of a door opening for me to leave.

I knew then that I had to choose myself, my safety, and my peace of mind. The decision to leave wasn't easy; it wasn't something I wanted to do. But I couldn't keep living in a situation that was literally destroying me, body and soul. I had to break free, for the sake of my daughter, for my own sanity, and for my future.

Hospitalization and a Long Recovery

I was finally able to file for divorce, but by the time I did, my body was in such a state of collapse that I was hospitalized for more than fifty-two days. My joints were infected, my body swollen and weak, and I couldn't even perform the most basic tasks for myself. I had been carrying the weight of my broken marriage for so long that it felt like my very spirit had shattered along with it. It wasn't just the physical toll; it was the emotional and mental strain that had worn me down to

99

the bone. The life I had known as Mrs. Richardson, the life I had so desperately tried to hold together, was gone. I was no longer that woman. The name "Mrs. Richardson" had no place in my world anymore.

When I signed the divorce papers, it felt as though I was signing away my entire identity. All those years of trying to make things work, trying to build a life for my daughter and me, were gone in an instant. The name "Mrs. Richardson" felt like a foreign title, one that no longer belonged to me, but rather to a ghost of a life I had lived, a life marked by pain and disillusionment. I had poured everything into that marriage, only to be left with nothing but memories of broken promises. It felt like the storm that had raged inside me for years had finally torn everything apart, and in its wake, there was nothing left but the wreckage of who I had been.

But as I lay in the hospital, struggling to regain control of my body, I also had to face the emotional wreckage. I was no longer "Mrs. Richardson." Who was I now? What was left of me after everything that had happened? My identity had been so tightly intertwined with my role as a wife that it felt like I was losing myself all over again. The person I had been, strong, dedicated, loving, seemed lost in the devastation of a marriage that had destroyed me in ways I had never imagined.

It was during those long, lonely days in the hospital that I began to realize the enormity of what I had been through. The divorce, the physical breakdown, the mental exhaustion, it had all been part of a process, a cleansing, even though it didn't feel like it at the time. I had thought that if I left, I would be nothing, that somehow my worth had been tied up in being Mrs. Richardson. But as the days passed and my body slowly began to heal, I started to see that I wasn't nothing. I was someone who had endured a great deal of pain, and through it all, I was still standing.

My daughter, who was now a senior in high school, needed me more than ever, and my family stepped in to help care for her. They were my lifeline, offering the support I so desperately needed. I couldn't have gotten through that period without them. They made sure my daughter stayed on track in school, and while I was recovering, they stepped in to handle things that I couldn't. I was broken, but not completely lost. Slowly, I began to see that the woman I was, without the title of "Mrs. Richardson," was still valuable, strong, and still worthy of a future.

The storm was far from over, but God was carrying me through it. And in those quiet moments of recovery, I began to understand that my identity was not defined by the man I had been married to. It was defined by who I was in God's eyes. The road ahead was uncertain, but I was no longer bound by the name I had once clung to.

The Emotional Shift

The discharge from the hospital came the day after Thanksgiving. My uncle and aunt, who had traveled from Flint, Michigan, took me home, and with their support, I left the sterile walls of the hospital behind. But the emotional weight of that moment was heavy. It wasn't just the physical recovery I had to contend with; it was the profound shift in my identity. I had gone from being Mrs. Richardson, an identity I had held for years, to simply me. I was no longer someone's wife. I was now a single woman, and the emotional process of making that transition was overwhelming.

It was as though I had lived in the storm for so long that I had forgotten what calm felt like. But now, in the stillness, I could begin to see the clouds in my life slowly moving away. I could feel the faint stirrings of strength returning, a small flicker of hope in the darkness. God had carried me through this painful, difficult time, and though my body still bore the scars of the past, I was beginning to live again. The storm hadn't passed, but for the first time, I felt like I could weather it.

The Road to Recovery

The recovery was long and difficult. I was cared for by a nurse in the family, and each day felt like a battle, physically and emotionally. It was a slow process. Every small movement, every simple task felt monumental. But amid the pain, moments were fleeting, precious moments of peace. It was as though the storms that had raged within me for so long were finally starting to calm. The winds of fear and exhaustion were dying down, and for the first time in a while, I could breathe.

However, as the physical pain began to ease, a different storm began to brew within me, one of isolation. I had just moved from Mansfield, Louisiana, to Shreveport, and the weight of my new life settled in like a heavy fog. I felt so alone, so removed from everything I had known. The floodwaters of grief that had surged through my marriage and the end of my first marriage were still high, and I couldn't shake the memories. They lingered, flooding my mind in the quiet moments. The life I had built had shattered, and now, everything felt foreign.

I didn't want to see anyone. I didn't want to talk to anyone. The storm of isolation began to take root in my heart. I withdrew into myself, unsure of what the future would bring or if I was even strong enough to face it. The wind carried the echoes of my past, and I began to question everything about who I was now and what was left of the woman I had once been.

The Unexpected Invitation

Then, one day, my godsister called. She told me she knew someone who, like me, couldn't walk. He had endured his own trials, his own battles with health, and she believed that meeting him might make a difference in my life. At first, I dismissed it. I didn't want to meet anyone, whether male or female; it didn't matter. I was in a place where I couldn't bear the thought of opening myself up to anyone, especially someone who could remind me of the physical limitations I was still struggling with. I had become a prisoner of my own body, trapped in a state of constant recovery and uncertainty, and I couldn't fathom meeting someone who might ask me to confront that reality.

But my godsister kept insisting. She spoke with such conviction, urging me to meet this person, to listen to his story. "You don't have to say much," she said. "Just hear him out. His journey could change your perspective, help you see things in a new light." She didn't give up. She continued to call, continued to encourage me, week after week, until finally, after much resistance, I agreed.

At that moment, I had no idea that this meeting would mark the beginning of a shift in my life, a turning point in my recovery. I had been so consumed by my own pain, by the weight of the past, that I had lost sight of the possibility that someone else might have a story that could heal me, too. I agreed to meet him, still unsure of what to expect, but I was willing to take the first step.

When he arrived, I was caught off guard. He was nothing like what I had imagined. He had a calm, steady presence, a kind demeanor, and a strength that seemed to emanate from him despite his own physical challenges. The man who walked in was not the one I had expected. He wasn't defined by his inability to walk, but by his resilience, his courage, and his unwavering faith. He told me his story, not with sorrow or self-pity, but with a quiet dignity. He spoke of the struggles he had faced in his own life, the physical limitations he had overcome, and the grace he had found through it all. There was a light in his eyes that I hadn't seen in a long time. It was the kind of light that comes from a person who has weathered their own storms and emerged on the other side stronger, more whole.

I sat there, listening to him, and for the first time in a long time, I felt a flicker of hope. His story was not just one of survival; it was one of triumph. He had found a way to live fully, even with the physical challenges he faced. And in his words, I heard something I hadn't heard in myself for a long time: the possibility of peace, of healing, of joy even in the midst of hardship. I realized then that his story wasn't just about his journey; it was about the way God had carried him through, just as He had carried me through my own storms.

The more he spoke, the more I began to understand. I had been so focused on my own suffering, so fixated on my limitations, that I had forgotten what it meant to live fully, to embrace life despite the pain. His words were a reminder that there was still so much left to live for, so much to be grateful for, even when the road was hard.

When he finished, I felt something shift within me. It was as if a dam had broken inside my heart, and the floodgates of hope and healing began to pour in. This meeting, this man, his story had changed something in me. I realized that recovery wasn't just about healing my body. It was about healing my spirit, about rediscovering who I was outside of the storms that had defined me for so long.

In the weeks that followed, he continued to support me in ways I hadn't expected. He reached out to my pastor, the mission sisters at church, and even his niece, a cosmetologist, to help me with things I hadn't been able to do for myself. His actions were selfless, generous, and unexpected, and each gesture served as a reminder that healing was possible not just for the body but for the heart.

By the time I made it to church with his help, it felt as if the sun had begun to break through the clouds. The congregation prayed with me, and I was consumed with the Holy Spirit in a way I hadn't felt in years. I felt God's presence in that room like I hadn't before, like He was carrying me, holding me in His arms, ready to bring me to a new place of peace.

That moment, that meeting, changed everything for me. It was the beginning of a new chapter in my healing journey, one that reminded me that there was still life to be lived, joy to be found, even in the aftermath of so much pain.

Chapter 10

Love After the Calm

As I continued recovering from the trials that had tried to break me, he began showing up in ways that were small enough to overlook but steady enough to feel. His presence didn't demand attention; it simply existed, quiet and reassuring, like a soft light glowing in the corner of a dim room. I wasn't used to that kind of gentleness. I wasn't used to someone noticing my exhaustion or the hollow places grief had carved out in me. For so long, I had survived by standing strong on my own two feet, even when those feet were trembling. Yet here he was, offering me a steadiness I didn't know how to accept, offering help without strings, presence without pressure.

He would ask simple questions so simple that, at first, I brushed them off as ordinary courtesy. "Are you resting?" "Did you eat today?" "Are you feeling any better?" But the way he asked them, with sincerity softening every syllable, made them echo inside me long after he left the room. They were the kinds of questions that touched places I hadn't tended to in years, the kinds that reminded me that care did not have to be loud to be powerful. For the first time in a long time, I felt seen, not as someone who needed to be strong, but as someone who was allowed to be healing.

Then one day, he asked if he could help me get back on my feet. I remember the moment clearly, the quiet earnestness in his voice, the hesitant hope tucked behind his offer. At first, I didn't understand his motive. My mind was still wrapped in surviving, not dreaming, still sorting through the pieces of my life after the painful divorce that had left me scraped raw. My heart was tender in ways I didn't speak out loud. Romance wasn't just unappealing; it felt impossible. I told him no when he finally admitted that he felt something more than friendship. I didn't say it harshly; I simply spoke from a place that believed love, for me, had already run its course.

I thought I was done with all that. I thought I had reached the age, the wisdom, the weariness where love no longer made sense. I told myself I was stable, steadfast, unmovable. But truthfully, those words were armor I built because I didn't want to risk breaking again. I didn't want to hope again. Hope can be heavier than grief when you're afraid of losing it.

But he didn't retreat. He didn't push either. He just stayed steady, patient, gentle. He showed up in the same quiet ways he always had, asking about my day, offering a helping hand when I needed one, knowing when to give me space and when to simply sit nearby in silence. He didn't try to pull me into anything before I was ready. He didn't try to convince me of anything. He just allowed me to breathe.

And slowly, very slowly, I learned that his kindness came from a place of understanding. It wasn't until later that I learned he was walking through his own valley, carrying the scars of his own ending. He, too, had emerged from a broken marriage, his heart bruised in places he didn't always speak of. Suddenly, the way he moved with such gentleness made sense. His tenderness wasn't weakness; it was experience. It was empathy born from pain. He knew what it was to lose. He knew what it was to start again when you felt beyond starting.

Over time, my walls began to soften, not because he pushed them down, but because his presence made them unnecessary. He never asked me to heal faster than I could. He never tried to fill the spaces grief had carved out. He simply made room for me to rest, to breathe, to rediscover myself in the quiet safety of companionship.

That is how our relationship began, not in dramatic confessions or blazing passion, but in the slow, steady unfolding of two wounded hearts learning how to trust again. It began in the small spaces between conversations, in the shared silences, in the moments when kindness overshadowed fear.

And with time, we married. It wasn't rushed, and it wasn't forced. It was a step taken after many steps of healing and reflection, a promise made with sober hearts and clear understanding. Together, we stepped into a new season, hoping it would be filled with peace, faith, and a gentle kind of love that one built not on sparks but on endurance. One built on two hearts that had weathered storms and still believed, somehow, in sunlight.

A New Season of Light

Our nine years of marriage held their own kind of quiet beauty, nothing extravagant or dramatic, just a steady warmth that settled into the corners of our lives like sunlight through open curtains. After everything we had both survived before finding each other, that simplicity felt like a blessing in itself. Life finally moved at a gentler pace. We laughed more freely, breathed more deeply, and allowed ourselves to trust the peace that had finally arrived.

During those nine years, my daughter married, stepping confidently into her own new chapter. Not long after, she placed the title of "Grandmother" into my hands, though I didn't fully understand how that word would reshape my heart until the moment I saw my first grandson's tiny face. Then came the second, completing a joy I didn't even know I had room for. Those boys became the heartbeat of our family, little bursts of energy, curiosity, and pure innocence that filled every room they entered.

And he adored them. Absolutely adored them. From the moment he first held them, something softened in him, something deep and tender. They didn't share his blood, yet you would never have known it. They called him "Paw Paw," a name that seemed to melt him every time it slipped from their small voices. His whole face would light up in a way that no one else could evoke, as if that simple nickname

108

awakened a part of him that had been waiting quietly for years. The boys would run into his arms, and he would kneel to catch them, laughing with a joy that rose straight from the soul.

In those moments, watching them together, I often thought about how love can build families just as strongly as blood can sometimes be even stronger. He stepped into that role with no hesitation, no fear, no uncertainty. Just love. And the boys returned it to him without question.

For a long, precious stretch of time, the sky over our home remained clear. No storms, no shadows, just warm days, gentle nights, and the steady hum of a life that finally felt safe. We settled into that sweetness as if it would last forever. We believed in the quietness of it, trusted the stillness, allowed ourselves to exhale after years of holding breath.

It was a season we never imagined would end, a season so soft and golden that we didn't see the gathering clouds on the horizon.

The Storm That No Prayer Could Stop

The storm of health issues began to build, and slowly, painfully, he was getting sicker and sicker. It felt as though the wind was blowing harder each day, and the lightning was flashing through every part of our lives, with hospital visits coming back-to-back. I kept wondering what it would take for him to be healed. I had seen God carry me through storms before, and I trusted sometimes desperately that He would carry me through this one, too. The faith I had in God was the only thing I could lean on.

During this time, the grandsons were living with us, and they helped the sun shine a little brighter through the storm. He loved them fiercely, and they loved him right back, calling him "Paw Paw." Their laughter softened the heaviness in our home, even as his strength continued to fade.

The Last Echo of His Struggle

Then came the day he was discharged from yet another hospital stay, and although he was finally home, there was a heaviness in the air that I could not shake. He moved slowly through the house, each step revealing how much the illness had taken from him. Not long after he settled in, the nurse arrived to begin his physical therapy. The moment she stepped through the door and saw him, her expression shifted from routine professionalism to alarm. She didn't even need to examine him closely; the weakness in his body was visible, the frailty unmistakable. She told him bluntly without hesitation that he was far too weak, that he should never have been discharged, and that he needed to go back to the hospital immediately. She spoke as someone who had seen this kind of decline many times, someone who knew danger when she saw it. She insisted that she would send him back herself, that he had no business trying to recover at home in that condition.

But he shook his head. He replied quietly yet firmly, with a tired kind of determination, "I'm not going." And he didn't go. His refusal hung in the air like a cloud gathering itself before a storm, silent but powerful. Something in him had already made up its mind, and no amount of urging or pleading could move him from the place he had settled into within himself.

Later that afternoon, I noticed something different in his behavior. He seemed unsettled, as though his thoughts were drifting through fog he could no longer push aside. He asked unusual questions, ones that made me realize his mind was slipping into a space none of us could reach. He asked where my godson was, and I told him gently that he was in the den sleeping. He nodded, though I couldn't tell if my answer truly reached him.

A few minutes later, the phone rang. The sound startled him, and he rose from the living room, moving with a suddenness that surprised me, given how weak he had been. He walked toward the bedroom, and

I watched him disappear down the hallway. Only a few seconds passed, barely enough time for me to process his movement, before I heard a sound. It was sharp, heavy, unnatural. At first, my mind tried to make sense of it, telling me it must have been a fall, that he had simply lost his balance in his weakened state.

I stood up and hurried toward the bedroom. But before I could even reach the doorway, the truth hit me not through sight, but through scent. The air was filled with the unmistakable, searing smell of gunpowder. In that instant, the world around me collapsed. It felt as though the sky inside my soul had split open, releasing a violent downpour of grief that struck from every direction. I could barely breathe as the reality crashed into me: the illness that had plagued him, the cruel and relentless companion that had followed him for so long, had driven him to a desperate decision that shattered my world in a single moment.

His final act became the most wrenching loss I had ever known. The storm of his sickness had not only taken my husband it had redefined the very meaning of grief.

The Valley I Never Expected to Walk

In the days that followed, I found myself wandering through a labyrinth of sorrow and shame, trying to make sense of a loss that felt too heavy for any human heart to carry. I tried with everything in me to uphold the dignity of his memory, even as I worked quietly to shield our loved ones from the truth of how he passed. The burden grew sharper and heavier because of my grandsons. They had loved him with a pure, childlike devotion, and his sudden, tragic passing tore the security right out of their young world. Their confusion, their tears, their silence, all of it carved deeper wounds in my spirit. More than anything, I wanted his memory to remain a blessing, not a wound that reopened every time his name was spoken.

Yet even in the darkest corners of that catastrophic tragedy, God carried me. When my knees were too weak to hold me up, He stood for me. When my voice trembled, He whispered strength into places I thought were shattered beyond repair. And when grief tried to drown me, He lifted my head above the storm. The same God who had walked me through every trial before did not fail me in this one.

PART FIVE
THE FINAL STORMS

Chapter 11

The Unbelievable Love of My Third Marriage

Love returned to me most unexpectedly. It did not rush in with excitement or shake my world the way I once thought love had to. It came softly, quietly, like sunlight rising without being asked. I did not know I was ready for love again, and I did not go searching for it. It simply found its way into the broken, healing places of my heart where I had been learning to breathe again.

My life had already been shaped by the two marriages that came before. Those chapters were not wasted pages. They held real emotions, real lessons, real meaning. Each one taught me something about who I was, and each one opened my eyes a little more to the strength that God had been building in me over the years. By the time he entered my life, I had lived through storms that left marks on my spirit, but I had also learned what kind of peace my soul longed for.

He did not try to replace a single memory from my past. He did not compete with anything I had lived through. He understood that my story did not begin with him, and he respected that in a way that made me feel safe. From the beginning, he carried himself with a calmness that allowed me to breathe without fear that I had to rush my healing or pretend I had no scars. His presence was steady, and because of that, I slowly realized I could trust the ground beneath my feet again.

The remarkable thing about this love was how naturally it unfolded. It didn't force itself into my life. It didn't demand attention or urgency. It just showed up, day by day, moment by moment, with a kind of gentleness that reminded me God was still guiding my steps. And in that gentleness, I found the courage to let my heart open again.

Not because the past had been erased, but because this new season of my life welcomed the woman I had become.

There was no comparison between this love and what came before. Every chapter in my life carried its own purpose. This one simply arrived at a time when I needed a different kind of peace, one shaped by maturity, faith, and a deeper understanding of myself. And as I walked through each day with him, I felt God reminding me that love does not always come fast or loud. Sometimes it comes quietly, exactly when your spirit is ready for it.

The Healing That Grew Through Family

One of the most unbelievable parts of my third marriage was how naturally he stepped into my world. He didn't walk in trying to change anything about me. He didn't try to take away the scars that life had left behind. Instead, he accepted them as part of who I was. He understood that loving me meant understanding where I had been, and he never made me feel like those chapters were something to hide or rush past. His understanding allowed my heart to soften in ways I didn't even expect.

My grandsons were one of the greatest blessings in my life, and they had gone through their own storms. They didn't need a new figure trying to replace anything or anyone. What they needed was someone who could bring stability, patience, and a gentle presence. That was exactly what he offered them. He never tried to force a bond or step into a role that didn't belong to him. He allowed the boys to come to him at their own pace, and the connection that formed was something God clearly had His hand in.

Our home didn't fill with grand gestures or big speeches. It was filled with small things that mattered warmth of shared meals, the laughter that came back into the rooms, the quiet moments when peace settled over all of us. Healing was happening without anyone announcing it. It grew through the simple routines of life, through evenings spent together, through the steady feeling of comfort that wrapped around us when we least expected it.

There were still times when old pains resurfaced. That's what happens when love has been through storms. Something small would stir up a memory or an ache from long ago, and I would feel myself slipping back toward the places I thought I had already moved past. But instead of judgment or questioning, he responded with patience. Not in a dramatic way, but calmly and steadily, that reminded me that I did not have to walk through those moments alone.

He never made me feel like I needed to pretend or hide the emotional weather that sometimes rose inside me. He treated my experiences as meaningful parts of who I was. And because of that, I learned to let go of certain fears that had been lingering in my heart. He didn't remove the storms from my life, but he stood beside me through each one, and that gave me strength I didn't realize I still had.

What surprised me most was how our love felt natural, not as a replacement for what came before, and not as a correction to past mistakes. It felt like a continuation, a new season that grew from everything I had lived through. It was not "more love." It was simply a different kind of love one that belonged to who I was in this chapter of my life. And that was enough to bring peace back into my days in a way I had not felt in a long time.

A Marriage Shaped by God's Timing

Looking back on my third marriage, I can see God's timing woven through every part of it. Nothing felt rushed, and nothing felt forced. It was the kind of relationship that grew naturally, almost quietly, until I realized it had become an anchor in my life. After everything I had lived through, I didn't need a love that overwhelmed me. I needed a love that brought peace, steadiness, and understanding; that is exactly what God placed in my life.

Our marriage was filled with simple moments that carried a deeper meaning. We had our share of challenges, just like any couple, but what carried us through was the calmness we brought to each other. He didn't need big gestures to prove anything. What mattered were the everyday acts of care, the support that showed up in ordinary moments, and the way we built a home that felt safe for both of us.

He knew I had lived through storms. He knew my heart carried memories and pains that were not instantly healed. Instead of stepping around those things, he acknowledged them as part of the woman he loved. He once told me that he understood he was choosing all of the strong parts, the hurting parts, the hopeful parts, and even the parts still learning to trust again. That acceptance helped me relax into the kind of love I hadn't believed I would experience again.

There were times when I felt another storm rising inside me, moments when the "not knowing" stirred up fear. But every time those emotions surfaced, I remembered how many storms God had already carried me through. And just as He had done before, He carried me through this season as well. The unbelievable love in this marriage didn't remove my challenges simply made them easier to walk through.

This marriage reminded me that nothing in my life had been wasted. Every chapter, every memory, every heartbreak, and every lesson had shaped me into the woman I was when God brought this love into my life. My past did not disappear simply found its place in a larger story. And in this chapter, I discovered that love could feel peaceful, steady, and deeply comforting without needing to be compared to anything that came before.

When I think of the life we shared, I feel grateful. Not because this love was louder or greater, but because it was right for the woman I had become. It was love that matched the healing God had placed in my heart. It was love that gave me the strength to understand that every chapter of my life had a purpose. And for that, I will always be thankful.

Chapter 12

The Season of Losses

I thought I had walked through my last storm. After everything God had already carried me through, after the healing that had finally come, I believed the hardest seasons were behind me. My third marriage had brought a peace I didn't know was possible, and I had settled into a life that felt steady and safe. But life does not always honor the peace we think we have earned. Sometimes, when we least expect it, the storms return not to punish us, but to reveal the strength we didn't know we still had to find.

This chapter of my life did not unfold the way I thought it would. It was supposed to be the season of rest, the reward for all the hard lessons I had learned. Instead, it became the season where everything I thought I understood about endurance was tested in ways I could never have imagined. The storms that came were not like the ones before. They were deeper, heavier, and more relentless. And they did not come one at a time. They came in waves that crashed over me so fast I could barely catch my breath between them.

The peace I had built began to crack under the weight of what I was facing. But even as the cracks appeared, I learned something that would carry me through every dark moment ahead. I learned that peace is not the absence of storms. Peace is knowing that God is present in the storm, even when you cannot feel Him, even when you cannot see the way forward, and even when your body and spirit are so tired that you wonder if you have anything left to give.

The Storm of Physical Betrayal

The first battle I faced in this season was one I never expected to fight. It was not with the world around me or with the people in my life. It was with my own body. My skin, the very surface that had carried me through every chapter of my life, began to turn against me. What started as a small concern grew into a relentless medical condition that would not let go. It demanded attention, it demanded strength, and it demanded more from me than I thought I had left to offer.

The doctors explained what was happening, but their words felt distant and unreal. Surgery after surgery followed. Not just one or two, but more than twenty over the years. Each one brought its own pain, its own recovery, its own challenge to face. And just when I thought I had healed enough to move forward, another procedure would be scheduled, another battle would begin, and I would find myself back in the hospital, staring at ceilings I had memorized, praying for strength I wasn't sure I still had.

The physical pain was overwhelming. It settled into my bones and stayed there, a constant companion that never fully left. Even on the days when I felt stronger, the pain reminded me of what my body had been through. It was exhausting in a way that went beyond tiredness. It drained something deeper, something in my spirit that I couldn't name but could feel slipping away with each passing month.

I tried to hold onto the peace I had found in my marriage, but the storms were relentless. They washed over everything, leaving no part of my life untouched. The simple routines that had once brought comfort became difficult to maintain. The laughter that had filled our home grew quieter. The strength I thought I had rebuilt began to crumble under the weight of chronic pain and endless medical procedures.

There were nights when I lay awake, unable to sleep because of the pain, and I asked God why this was happening. I had already walked through so much. I had already survived things I never thought I would survive. Why was there more? Why, after finally finding peace, did the storms return with even greater force? I did not always hear an answer, but I kept asking. Because even in my confusion, even in my exhaustion, I knew that God was the only one who could carry me through this.

When the Ground Gave Way

The medical storm was not the only challenge I faced. As my body weakened, other parts of my life began to shift in ways I couldn't control. The woman I had been, the one who had learned to stand strong, who had found her voice, who had rebuilt her life from broken pieces, felt like she was slipping away. I didn't recognize myself in the mirror some days. The surgeries had changed me, not just physically, but in ways that went deeper than what anyone could see.

I struggled to hold onto the identity I had worked so hard to build. The pain made it difficult to be present with the people I loved. My grandsons needed me, and I wanted to be there for them the way I had always been, but some days I simply couldn't. The exhaustion was too great. The pain was too constant. And the guilt I felt for not being enough weighed on me almost as heavily as the physical burden I was carrying.

My husband stood beside me through all of it. He never wavered, never complained, never made me feel like I was a burden. But I saw the worry in his eyes. I felt the weight he was carrying as he watched me go through procedure after procedure, recovery after recovery, with no clear end in sight. He did everything he could to help me, to comfort me, to remind me that I was not walking through this alone. And yet, there were moments when I felt completely isolated in my pain, moments when no one, not even him, could reach the place inside me where the storm raged the loudest.

The loss that came at the end of this storm was one I never imagined I would have to face. My toes, ten pieces of my body that I had never thought twice about, were taken from me. The medical condition had progressed to a point where there was no other option. And in losing them, I lost more than just physical parts of myself. I lost a sense of wholeness I didn't realize I needed. I lost the ability to walk the way I once had, to move through the world without thinking about every step. I lost something that felt like the final piece of who I used to be.

The Woman Who Emerged

But here is what I learned in the fire of that season. I learned that what defines us is not what we lose. It is how we choose to stand after the loss. I learned that strength is not about never breaking, it is about finding the courage to keep breathing even after you have been broken. I learned that God's presence is not always loud or obvious. Sometimes it is quiet, woven into the smallest mercies a moment of relief from pain, a kind word from someone who cares, the ability to wake up one more day and choose to keep going.

The woman who emerged from this storm is not the same woman who entered it. She carries scars that will never fully fade. She walks differently now, moves through the world with a new awareness of her own fragility. But she also carries something else, a fierce, unshakable will to survive. A refusal to let the storms define the end of her story. A quiet certainty that God has carried her this far, and He will carry her through whatever comes next.

The love I found in my third marriage taught me things I did not know I needed to learn. His steadiness showed me that I could be steady too. His patience reminded me to be patient with myself when my body took longer to heal than I wanted. His presence helped me see that I was still whole, even after losing parts of myself I thought I needed.

What he gave me became part of who I am now. The bravery I learned through him is mine to keep. The strength that grew during those hard years belongs to me. I do not lean on his love to survive anymore. Instead, I carry what it taught me, and that is enough to keep me standing.

Chapter 13

The Physical Losses: A War on the Body

There are moments in life when suffering becomes so heavy, so relentless, that it carves a permanent place within you. I had already lived through heartbreak, disappointment, and emotional storms that reshaped the deepest parts of my soul. But nothing prepared me for the season when my own body would turn into a battlefield. Physical pain is a different kind of trial. It doesn't negotiate. It doesn't soften just because you have already endured enough. It arrives with its own mission, its own timing, and its own ache that seeps into every corner of your life.

At first, I didn't understand what was happening. A small discomfort here, a little swelling there, things I brushed aside because life was already filled with responsibilities and moments that needed my attention. But illnesses have a way of whispering before they roar. Before long, the whispers grew louder, and the reality I once stood on began to shift beneath my feet. What I thought would be a passing issue became a life-altering condition that swept me into a cycle of procedures, hospital beds, and endless recovery rooms.

In time, I would face more than twenty surgeries. Each one was its own chapter, filled with its own fears and hopes. I learned the layout of hospital corridors the way some people learn the streets of their hometowns. I could recognize the sound of machines in the dark, and I knew how it felt to wait for doctors to enter a room with answers I wasn't always ready to hear. Pain settled into my days like an unwelcome companion, one that followed me from morning to night without giving me space to breathe. Yet somehow, through each operation, I held on to the belief that God had not brought me this far to abandon me.

A Loss That Shaped My Steps Forever

Out of every physical blow I endured, the most devastating came in the slow deterioration of my feet. They had carried me through every season of my life. Through childhood, motherhood, marriages, heartbreaks, and new beginnings, my feet had never once failed me. I trusted them without thinking, without appreciating the miracle of simply standing or walking.

But illness brings everything into focus. It forces you to notice the things you once dismissed. My feet began to ache in ways I could not describe. The pain was sharp at first, then grew into a constant throb that made every step feel heavier than the last. I held on to hope that treatment would help, that medication would work, that prayers would carry me through. And while prayers always sustained me, my condition continued to decline.

The day the doctors told me the truth, *your toes cannot be saved,* a silence fell over me. It wasn't dramatic. It wasn't loud. It was the kind of silence that comes when your spirit tries to understand what your mind cannot yet grasp. The idea of amputation felt like something that could not belong to my life, yet there it was, standing in front of me, unavoidable.

When the surgery happened, it felt like more than a procedure. It felt like a grieving. A part of me had been taken, and even though I knew it was necessary, it did not make the loss easier. Losing my toes was not simply a physical change; it was an emotional earthquake. I had to learn how to walk again, not just with my body but with my heart. Every step afterward reminded me of what I had lost and what I was learning to accept. Balance became something I had to fight for, physically and emotionally.

There is a vulnerability that comes with losing a piece of your body. It humbles you. It softens you. It teaches you to appreciate every movement, every shift of weight, every moment on your feet. And in the midst of that vulnerability, a quiet strength began to grow in me, one that came not from what I had left, but from what I still refused to surrender.

Love That Stood in the Darkness Beside Me

During this painful chapter, my third husband became a source of strength I never expected. He had already brought peace and comfort into my life in ways that healed my emotional wounds, but the love he showed during my physical suffering revealed a depth I had never known before. He did not walk away from the confusion, the fear, or the exhaustion. Instead, he stepped closer.

He became my caregiver long before either of us was ready for what that meant. Loving someone through illness is not glamorous or easy. It is a daily commitment. It is patience. It is compassion that renews itself every morning. He learned how to change dressings with a gentleness that still brings tears to my eyes. He helped me stand when I could not find my balance. He listened when pain made me quiet, and he stayed awake when my nights were filled with discomfort instead of rest.

There were moments when I felt helpless, moments when I wondered if I had become a burden. But every time that fear tried to swallow me, he reminded me, without even needing to say it, that love is built for more than good days. He never flinched at the responsibility of helping me through surgeries, recovery, and the emotional storms that rose inside me. He chose to be present, consistently, faithfully, even when the situation became exhausting.

He never treated my illness as something that separated us. Instead, he treated it as something we were facing together. When frustration overwhelmed me, he did not respond with irritation but with understanding. When sadness washed over me, he gave me space without distance. And when I needed strength but had none left to offer, he willingly lent me his.

This kind of love is not loud. It is not dramatic or decorated with grand gestures. It is a quiet, persistent loyalty, the kind that holds you together when your body feels like it is falling apart. He became the steady hand on my shoulder, the reassurance in my darkest hours, and the reminder that even in suffering, I was still cherished, still valued, still loved.

Grace That Carried Me Through the Storm

Even with my husband's unwavering care, there were moments no human could reach. Pain isolates you in a way that nothing else can. There were nights when I lay awake, silently praying because the ache felt too deep for words. Nights when fear crept into my thoughts, fear of what my body would face next, fear of losing more, fear of not being strong enough to continue.

In those moments, it was God who carried me.

His presence did not always come in dramatic signs. Most of the time, it came in small, quiet assurances, the kind that settle into your spirit when you're too weak to ask for miracles. I felt Him in the gentle shift of morning light after a painful night. I felt Him in the calm that washed over me before surgeries. I felt Him in the strength that appeared out of nowhere on days when I thought I could not take another step.

God did not stop the storm, but He taught me how to walk through it. He reminded me that my life still had purpose even when my body felt broken. He reminded me that loss does not erase strength. And He reminded me that survival can be just as divine as healing.

Looking back, I realize that every moment of suffering was shaping me in ways I didn't understand then. My body changed, but so did my heart. I learned compassion for others in pain. I learned humility. I learned resilience. And I learned that even in the hardest seasons, God does not let us face the battle alone.

I survived the surgeries, the losses, the fear, and the uncertainty not because I was stronger than the pain, but because God and the love around me carried me through it. Physical losses may have defined this chapter of my life, but it was also marked by an inner strength I never knew I had.

EPILOGUE
THE CARRYING CONTINUES

As I sit here today, writing these final words, I am not the same woman who began this story in the cotton fields of rural Louisiana. My hands, which once picked cotton under the punishing Southern sun, now rest gently on the pages of a completed manuscript. My feet, which once carried me through childhood storms and into adulthood's trials, are forever changed; ten toes gone, but my spirit still standing.

I am seventy-eight years old now. When I look in the mirror, I see a woman marked by time, by loss, by survival. The scars are visible; some on my body, some deeper still, carved into the places only God can see. But I also see something else: I see a woman who refused to stay down. I see a woman who learned that strength is not about never breaking; it is about choosing to stand again after you have been shattered.

The storms documented in these pages are behind me now, though their echoes still whisper through my days. I think of my son, David Jerome Brooks, every single day. Not with the crushing weight of fresh grief that once threatened to bury me, but with a bittersweet ache that has softened into sacred memory. He would have been in his fifties now. I wonder what kind of man he would have become, what dreams he would have chased, what grandchildren he might have given me. But I have learned to hold those questions with open hands, trusting that God's plan, even when it shatters my own, is still good.

My daughter is a woman of strength and grace, raising her own family with a resilience I recognize as both inherited and hard-won. My grandsons, who once called my third husband "Paw Paw," are growing into young men. They carry pieces of everyone who loved them: my mother's faith, my father's work ethic, my own stubborn refusal to quit. When I watch them, I see the legacy that survives every storm: *love that endures, faith that anchors, and strength that multiplies across generations.*

My mother, my father, my brother Junior, my grandmothers; they are all gone now, resting in the cemetery at New Hope Baptist Church. Sometimes, when I visit their graves, I sit quietly and tell them about my life. I tell them I made it. I tell them God carried me, just like they always said He would. And in the silence that follows, I feel their presence, a gentle assurance that the love we shared is not bound by death.

If I could distill everything I have learned into a single truth, it would be this: *You are stronger than you think, and you are never alone.*

The storms will come. That is not a possibility; it is a certainty. Life does not offer exemptions from suffering. The rain will fall, the wind will blow, the thunder will shake the foundations of everything you thought was solid. You will face losses that break your heart, illnesses that break your body, and disappointments that break your spirit. You will stand in the wreckage of your life and wonder how you will ever rebuild.

But here is what I know now, after weathering every storm documented in these pages: *The God who created the storm is also the God who carries you through it.*

The storms in my life did not destroy me. They refined me. They burned away everything that was temporary and revealed what was eternal. They taught me that joy is sweeter after sorrow, that peace is deeper after chaos, and that faith is strongest when it has been tested by fire.

Today, I live with chronic pain. My body is not what it used to be. I move more slowly, I tire more easily, and there are days when the physical limitations feel overwhelming. But I also live with a peace I never knew was possible. I wake up each morning grateful for another day, another breath, another chance to witness God's faithfulness.

I have learned to find joy in the small things: a grandchild's laughter, a sunrise after a long night, a phone call from a friend, the simple act of sitting in church and feeling the presence of God wash over me. These moments, which I once rushed past in my hurry to survive, are now the treasures I hold most dear.

The storms taught me to slow down, to pay attention, to savor the sunshine when it breaks through the clouds. Because the truth is, *the sunshine is always there, even when the clouds temporarily hide it.* And after you have walked through enough darkness, you learn to recognize light in places you never noticed before.

If you are tired, bone-deep, soul-tired, the kind of tired that sleep cannot fix, I see you. I have been you. I have lived in that exhaustion that makes every step feel like climbing a mountain.

But I am here to tell you that rest is coming. Maybe not today, maybe not tomorrow, but it is coming. The storm will not last forever. The sun will break through. The floodwaters will recede. And when they do, you will look back and realize that the same storm that threatened to destroy you actually prepared you for something greater.

You will emerge from this crucible stronger, wiser, and more compassionate. You will carry scars, yes, but those scars will become your testimony. They will be the proof that you survived, the roadmap you can offer to others who are lost in their own storms.

Your pain will not be wasted. God will use every tear you have cried, every prayer you have whispered, every moment you thought you could not go on. He will take the broken pieces of your life and create something beautiful. Not despite the storms, but because of them.

The title of this book is "God Carried Me," but the truth is, the carrying never stops. Even now, as I write these words, I am being carried. Every breath is a gift. Every morning is evidence of grace. Every step I take on feet that have been forever changed is a miracle of divine strength.

And just as God carried me, He is carrying you. Right now, in this very moment, even if you cannot feel it, *His hands are underneath you.* You are not falling. You are being held.

So, when the storms come, and they will come, remember this: You are not alone. You have never been alone. The God who counts the hairs on your head, who knows the number of your days, who collects every tear you cry, is walking with you through the darkness.

He will carry you through the fire, and you will not be burned.

He will carry you through the flood, and you will not drown.

He will carry you through the storm, and you will survive.

Not because you are strong enough on your own, but because His strength is made perfect in your weakness.

This is my testimony. This is my truth. And this is my prayer for you:

May you find the courage to surrender your burdens. May you discover the peace that surpasses understanding. May you experience the carrying that has sustained me through every storm. And may you emerge from your trials with a testimony that gives hope to others.

The storms are real. The pain is real. But so is the God who carries us through.

And that, dear reader, is the only truth that matters.

With all my love and faith,

—*Bertha*

Acknowledgment

First and foremost, I would like to thank God for His amazing grace and everlasting mercy. I thank Him for His direction and provision during the storms in my life.

I thank my parents, Douglas Brooks, Sr., and Queen Ester White Brooks, for the foundation they laid for me to follow. I would also like to thank Rachel Anderson for giving me the extra push to write my book, and Qutaywan Anderson for designing my book cover.

Special thanks to Kermerneshia and Amore for staying with me when I came home with an IV in my arm that had to be changed twice a day.

A very special thank you to Lisa Bedford, Pastor Ardis, and Apostle Jessical Haley for taking unbelievable care of me daily.

I thank my daughter, Bridget Richardson-Thomas, for giving me two grandsons, Vincent and Devin Hendricks. I thank Devin for his outstanding service as he protects and serves the United States of America in the Navy. I thank Vincent for blessing me with three beautiful great-granddaughters: Viola, Violet, and Ryleigh Hendricks. I also thank their mother, Richelle Green, for the unbelievable care she has dedicated to the girls.

I would like to thank my family and friends for their support.

Last but not least, I would like to thank my church families, New Hope Baptist Church and Lake Bethlehem Baptist Church, and their pastors, J. A. Reliford and Dennis R. Everett. I also extend my heartfelt gratitude to Ink Founder for their support when I felt like giving up, especially Hannah Collins, who worked diligently on my project and guided me through each phase with clarity and encouragement.

To God be the glory.

About The Author

Bertha, the author of *"God Carried Me: The Woman Who Had Many Storms, A Life of Rising,"* embodies the fierce spirit of endurance. Her story is one of profound heartbreak and ultimate triumph; a testament to faith and the will to survive.

Her journey spans three marriages: the first ending in necessary separation after abuse, the second concluding with her husband's tragic suicide, and the third revealing that redemptive love can emerge even after devastating loss. Through it all, she anchored her family, particularly her grandsons, through immense grief.

In her later years, she faced an unimaginable physical battle; more than twenty surgeries, and the amputation of all ten toes, while navigating the back-to-back deaths of her last brother and her third husband within six months.

A retired educator who spent decades lifting up struggling students, she now shares her testimony: even when the body is broken and the heart shattered, the spirit can rise. A life of rising is always possible.